Camelot in the Nineteenth Century

Recent Titles in
Contributions to the Study of World Literature

The Adventure of the Detected Detective: Sherlock Holmes in James Joyce's
Finnegans Wake
William D. Jenkins

Afro-Cuban Literature: Critical Junctures
Edward J. Mullen

The Tales We Tell: Perspectives on the Short Story
Barbara Lounsberry, Susan Lohafer, Mary Rohrberger, Stephen Pett, and
R. C. Feddersen, editors

Robin Hood: The Shaping of the Legend
Jeffrey L. Singman

The Myth of Medea and the Murder of Children
Lillian Corti

African-British Writings in the Eighteenth Century: The Politics of Race and Reason
Helena Woodard

Styles of Ruin: Joseph Brodsky and the Postmodernist Elegy
David Rigsbee

The Image of Manhood in Early Modern Literature: Viewing the Male
Andrew P. Williams, editor

The Worlding of Jean Rhys
Sue Thomas

Ulysses, Capitalism, and Colonialism
M. Keith Booker

Imperial Knowledge: Russian Literature and Colonialism
Ewa M. Thompson

Demythologizing the Romance of Conquest
Jeanne Armstrong

Camelot in the Nineteenth Century

Arthurian Characters in the Poems of Tennyson, Arnold, Morris, and Swinburne

Laura Cooner Lambdin
and Robert Thomas Lambdin

Contributions to the Study of World Literature, Number 97

GREENWOOD PRESS
Westport, Connecticut • London

Library of Congress Cataloging-in-Publication Data

Lambdin, Laura Cooner.
  Camelot in the nineteenth century : Arthurian characters in the
poems of Tennyson, Arnold, Morris, and Swinburne / Laura Cooner Lambdin
and Robert Thomas Lambdin.
    p.   cm.—(Contributions to the study of world literature,
ISSN 0738–9345; no. 97)
  Includes bibliographical references and index.
  ISBN 0–313–31124–2 (alk. paper)
  1. English poetry—19th century—History and criticism.
2. Arthurian romances—Adaptations—History and criticism.
3. Tennyson, Alfred Tennyson, Baron, 1809–1892—Knowledge—Arthurian
romances.   4. Swinburne, Algernon Charles, 1837–1909—Knowledge—
Arthurian romances.   5. Arnold Matthew, 1822–1888—Knowledge—
Arthurian romances.   6. Morris, William, 1834–1896—Knowledge—
Arthurian romances.   7. Medievalism—England—History—19th
century.   8. Knights and knighthood in literature.   9. Kings and
rulers in literature.   10. Middle Ages in literature.   11. Camelot
(Legendary place)   I. Lambdin, Robert Thomas.   II. Title.   III. Series.
PR595.A79L36   2000
821'.809351—dc21   99–21707

British Library Cataloguing in Publication Data is available.

Library of Congress Catalog Card Number: 99–21707
ISBN: 0–313–31124–2
ISSN: 0738–9345

First published in 2000

Greenwood Press, 88 Post Road West, Westport, CT 06881
An imprint of Greenwood Publishing Group, Inc.
www.greenwood.com

Printed in the United States of America

The paper used in this book complies with the
Permanent Paper Standard issued by the National
Information Standards Organization (Z39.48–1984).

10 9 8 7 6 5 4 3 2 1

To Our

Sweet Siblings

Jef, Debbi,

Marion, and John

Contents

Introduction

For centuries, accounts of King Arthur and his court have fascinated historians, scholars, poets, and readers. Legends of this powerful, commanding warrior, who was also the perfect monarch of tragic destiny, probably began as folk stories in Wales and Ireland. The Arthurian story remains with us because it has always been "common property, with no copyright and no prize for originality. Every author is an independent agent, but cannot work without his predecessors: he is a dwarf standing on the shoulders of a cumulative giant" (R. Morris 4). Each age added aspects that reflected its own cultural attitudes; however, no age supplemented the earlier versions more than the poets writing during the Medieval Revival of nineteenth-century England, a revival that embraced art, architecture, philosophy, economics, politics, sociology, and religion. The Medieval Revival had its origins in the Romantic movement's susceptibility to the beauty and intensity of medieval literature. Before this, between the Middle Ages and the rise of Romanticism, the classical spirit ruled and was by nature alien to medievalism.

The French Revolution brought rapid and frightening changes that conservative England wished to avoid. Post-Napoleonic attitudes toward the Middle Ages began with ideas of a charming, picturesque period stemming from Sir Walter Scott's preoccupation with the period's romantic and historical aspects. This early stage included reverence for a golden age of stability. Medieval society was idealized as one founded on faith and loyalty. Victorian writers who felt that their age was devoid of true spiritualism saw in the Middle Ages a good vehicle for explaining and analyzing contemporary life. Suddenly, a society searching for national identity and a means of making sense of disturbing, rapid changes developed a strong historical consciousness.

Gothic interests in medieval architectural style, such as Horace Walpole's Strawberry Hill Castle (1754-94), when combined with the Romantic desire for a more natural, organically ordered society, clashed with industrial values. Ugly factory buildings spewing smoke and miserably overworked, underfed workers made the current departure from the old ways of feudalism only too clear. Thomas Carlyle encouraged readers to "examine history, for it is Philosophy teaching by Experience" (*Works* 27:85); he rejected doctrines of progress, utilitarianism, and laissez-faire economics and longed for a return to the paternal leadership of feudalism or at least hoped to encourage manufacturers to take more responsibility for the conditions of their employees. This is medievalism with a purpose beyond a regret for the lost pastoral elements of rural England.

Many religious leaders also extolled the medieval period as a time when the church had more interaction with the community. The Middle Ages were seen as a period of faith, humanity, and prosperity under the rule of one great church; especially admired were the monasteries, which offered relief, advice, and protection to all. The early monks were revered as more active, sincere, mild, and studious than spiritual leaders of the present. Even the imagined moral qualities of chivalrous knights were thought to have benefited society.

The monarchy also had reason to promote this renewed interest in England's early history, when powerful rulers were not subject to the votes of Parliament. Queen Victoria and Prince Consort Albert especially adored Arthurian subjects; from 1849 to 1862 William Dyce painted frescoes in the Queen's Robing Room at the Palace of Westminster that represented men of the Round

Table as personified qualities of mercy, hospitality, generosity, religion, courtesy, fidelity, and courage.

This type of visual personification was reflected and enlarged by nineteenth-century poets, who went beyond Scott's romances of the chivalry of "Merrie" England to find metaphors for the human spirit in the historical or legendary past. Victorian poets not only dreamed of a period rendered more attractive by distance, but were also interested in authenticity of spirit. Enchanted castles, magic forests, evil dwarfs, cruel giants, and distressed damsels, the trappings of medieval romances so embraced by Gothic writers were of less significance. Themes of defense and conquest were eroded by the Grail Quest and its Christian message. No other medieval literature could reflect feelings of contemporary unrest as well as the tragic legends of Arthur, Guinevere, Lancelot, Merlin, Tristram, Iseult, and the whole host of Arthurian characters whose lives were shattered by a failed ideal. Each of the nineteenth-century English poets who studied and then rewrote the ancient Arthurian legends left his feelings about his own society just under the surface of poetry extolling the medieval period.

Perhaps the reconstruction of a historical moment can explain poetic choices, but a great variety of thought is possible within a culture sharing common concerns. The importance of both individual and universal aspects is reinforced when we realize that "the Arthurian Grail legend is both timeless and contemporaneous, with a protean capacity to reinforce the aspirations and respond to the aesthetic, moral, and spiritual needs of humankind in succeeding ages" (Lagorio and Day xi). We cannot deny the strength of human individuality and must realize that even though certain trends are prevalent in nineteenth-century British attitudes toward history, the enormous power of the Arthurian tragedy itself was likely to trigger intense emotional responses in such poets as Alfred Tennyson, Matthew Arnold, William Morris, and Algernon Charles Swinburne. The concentration of this study will be on the use by these four major nineteenth-century poets of the medieval versions of the Arthurian legend, most importantly the works of Sir Thomas Malory, and how these Victorian poets reflected their own views and influenced each other's conceptions of the lessons to be learned from the tragic tale of Arthur's court.

Although previous criticism has examined many aspects of Arthurian legend as it pertains to nineteenth-century social conditions, this study diverges from others in its approach. While other commentators' theories will be reviewed, the focus here is the poets' ways of approaching two distinct states of being: love and death. Clearly the two topics, the joy of life and the end of life, are subjects of lyric poetry in general, but they are also of great significance in Arthurian legend in terms of leitmotifs, justification of plot (propter hoc), and characterization. Further, Tennyson, Arnold, Morris, and Swinburne present meditations concerning love and death in specific fashions that are dissimilar to the point of incompatibility. This divergence in attitudes changes the import of the entire Arthurian story as well as the way in which the legend reflects each poet's reaction to medieval England, Victorian England, and the universal human condition.

Each chapter following the first, which briefly traces Arthurian legend from its inception, discusses a different author's specific use of the ancient story, beginning with Tennyson's concept that true love depends upon an admiration of character, a respect that results in trust. When this highest faith is shattered and death quickly follows, the feeling of emptiness stemming from the loss of an ideal is overwhelming, especially since it causes the disintegration of an entire kingdom.

Arnold's position is one of moderation; the idea seems to be that love should be neither passionate nor passive in order to be satisfying. Relationships should be deep, but temperate, so that the loss of a loved one produces neither debilitating agony nor only a mild melancholy.

Morris's focus is on the freshness of strong feeling and the reality of passion that shows the beauty of intense emotion. He concentrates on the difference between physical, earthly love and spiritual, heavenly love, in which the latter is superior, if only slightly. His descriptions of courtly love are devoid of overt morality, as the characters simply follow emotional impulses without vacillation. Morris's poems concerning religious love show a realistic questioning of the degree of saintliness required of one on earth to ensure inclusion in heaven after death.

A relentlessly fatalistic world destroyed by love, whether erotic, fraternal, or spiritual, is evident in Swinburne's Arthurian poems. The idolatrous passion of courtly love is a perfect vehicle for Swinburne's private mythology of love as a sadomasochistic enterprise involving a lover wrecked by an unquenchable desire; the only possible conclusion is a wish for death as a release from the torture of love, with decay as a final organic unity with the earth.

Love in nineteenth-century Arthurian legends sometimes reflects a static dichotomy of pious and bestial trends; this polarity may stem from the contemporary theory of Darwinian animalism juxtaposed with the understanding of England as a great and proper civilization, a feeling that had recently been underscored by British imperialism and the new science of history. This belies a concern with the true nature of mortal man, which in turn causes wonder about the nature of God. Conceptions of death depend somewhat upon the shades of gray each author sees between atheism and evangelicalism. Each author's handling of love and death themes reveals his views about the meaning of human existence. Proper names are spelled in each section as the particular author spelled them in his work being discussed.

Chapter 1

Arthurian Legends: Origins to the Nineteenth Century

To remind the reader of the early Arthurian legends, many of which were read by the four Victorian poets we discuss in this volume, we will briefly note the particular contributions of influential medieval writers. This cursory survey is intended only to show the Victorian point of departure from medieval texts. The focus is on the work of Thomas Malory, because Tennyson, Morris, and Swinburne all depended heavily upon his text. (Arnold may not have read Malory's work until after he had written his own Arthurian story, but he was familiar with parts of it.)

If there was a real King Arthur, he lived in the sixth or the seventh century a.d., a period from which we have collected little reliable data. The early information we have does not clearly mean "that he ever became 'king' of any part of Britain. His achievements as a warrior alone are mentioned, and all that we can gather besides from Welsh tradition only serves to emphasize the fact that his renown among the British people rested mainly upon his warlike prowess" (Jones 11). He may have been a Welsh guerrilla fighter who defended the English or one of the last Roman generals of Britain. The name Arthur is not Welsh, but probably transliterates he common Roman name *Arthurius*, so it seems likely that he was a Roman who helped the Celts against the Anglo-Saxons.

Arthur is first mentioned by name in a ninth-century chronicle, *Historia Brittonum* (c. 800), attributed to a Welsh historian named Nennius. In this revival of Welsh nationalism, Arthur is not a king, but a great warlord who pushes the British force to victory in twelve great battles; in one, the Battle of Badon Hill, Arthur kills 960 of the enemy by his own hand.

A later work, *Annales Cambriæ* (c. 950), is a brief, anonymous account that adds that Arthur fought in the Battle of Badon Hill for three days while bearing a cross of Christ on his shoulders. This chronicle also mentions that Arthur was killed at the Battle of Camlann (c. 539) along with a certain Medraut (who later becomes Mordred, the patricide).

There are other histories of this type that give little information about Arthur and read like newspaper headlines or outlines. Chronicles in the early twelfth century elaborated Arthur's story, using details from the firmly established Welsh and Irish folklore concerning the hero. The legend was also known by this time in France and northern Italy.

It was Geoffrey of Monmouth's *Historia Regum Britanniæ* (1136) that solidified the Arthurian legends and claimed an important place for them, as this fiction was taken as history by many generations of later writers well into the Renaissance. Geoffrey claimed to have translated an ancient book written in the English language that had been given to him by Walter, Archdeacon of Oxford. Few scholars believe in this source, inasmuch as citing such authorities was a standard ploy of medieval writers, although it is possible that Geoffrey may have had a written copy of ancient oral folklore. Many of the details, like the characters' names and the names of Arthur's weapons, can be traced to Welsh oral tradition.

Geoffrey's work is a patriotic history that gives the Anglo-Norman aristocracy a British hero/ruler as noble as Charlemagne. England is traced from the fall of Troy until Brutus flees to Britain. For the first time we see contemporary politics involved in an English chronicle: the Norman's interest in bringing Brittany into their sphere of influence is reflected in the large part that the Bretons play (Barber 10). There is also the possibility that Geoffrey intended Arthur's Roman expedition to reflect Henry V's conquest of France, as Rosemary Morris notes:

Henry was challenged in his own court by an insolent message; his counselors urged him to take up the challenge which he joyfully did; he crossed the channel, landing at Harfleur, swept through Northern France, fought a great battle and was hailed as king, but died before he could be crowned--all this Geoffrey's Arthur does--in the 1130's. (1)

Geoffrey is the first to record Arthur's conception as the product of Merlin's disguising Uther Pendragon as the Duke of Cornwall, the husband of Igerna. This echoes a similar tale in the romances about Alexander the Great. Arthur became a symbol of British national spirit and a practical model for medieval and Renaissance kings as well as an ideal for the people, a hero in touch with the latest fashions of courtly behavior.

Despite the many anachronisms this currency demanded, between 1150 and 1420 some fifty chroniclers used *Historia Regum Britanniæ* as the basis for other histories of England. A Norman clerk, Wace, wrote a poem in French based on Geoffrey's work; Wace called it the *Roman de Brut* (1154) and presented it to the wife of Henry II of England, Eleanor of Aquitaine. The poem contains the first extant mention of the Round Table, a piece of furniture introduced because Arthur's followers could not agree on a proper order of precedence as they sat down to meat.

The first English copy of Wace's *Roman de Brut* was Layamon's *Brut* (C. 1205), written by a Worcestershire priest. Layamon substituted the native alliterative meter for Wace's continental poetic form of octosyllabic couplets. The theme is the glory of Celtic Britain rather than Saxon England. Parts of the *Mabinogion* (1100-1250), a collection of early Welsh romances, elaborate Arthurian legend with two features typical of all the later stories: Arthur is ruler of the noblest court in the world and is involved, with his brave followers, in an assortment of marvelous adventures. The society depicted here is much more primitive than that of Geoffrey of Monmouth; the men hunt and fight on foot, rather than jousting in armor on enormous steeds. This Arthurian romance, untouched by the ideals of chivalry, deals only indirectly with the noble Arthur. It is, however, very important as so little native Welsh storytelling has survived, because their bards were reciting performers who did not record their work.

Although the Bretons were known for their talented minstrels, we have even less surviving material from them than we do from the Welsh. Breton lays are charming short fairy tales often set in Arthur's court, but barely mentioning him by name except as the "Breton hope," referring to the possible return of an Arthur who never died. These works involve much magic with some chivalry, as in *The Lay of Sir Launful* by Marie de France (1175), author of twelve Breton lays. *Launful* is one of her few Arthurian stories and reflects the reality of the court as a world of strife and jealousy, not nearly as appealing as the beautiful world of fairies.

The earliest extant long Arthurian romances are the elegant, artificial verses of the twelfth century Frenchman Chrétien de Troyes, who was associated with the court of Champagne and especially with the Countess Marie, the daughter of Eleanor of Aquitaine. Chrétien was concerned with the interlacing of court life, courtly love, and chivalry; he moved the exotic fairy tales of Welsh heroes into the castles of England and France. His surviving Arthurian works include *Erec et Enide* (c. 1170), *Lancelot* (c. 1179), *Yvain* (c. 1179), and *Perceval* (1180-90), all of which contain models of courtly behavior and polite conversation. For the first time, Chrtien combined all the essential ingredients of Arthurian romance. In England, French influence of this type resulted in the tale of *Sir Gawain and the Green Knight* (c. 1350). This poem represents the climax of English alliterative poetry and is the first poem to present Gawain, Arthur's nephew, as the primary hero.

From verse romances about individual heroes of Arthur's court, the French writers moved to prose, attempting to tell the whole history of Arthur, from his miraculous birth to his uncertain death. These writers became so caught up in complex digressions, frequently moral, that the story lines become difficult or impossible to follow or were even dropped entirely. Sir Thomas Malory's *Le Morte Darthur* was the first coherent, abbreviated version. This work reduces the French Arthurian legends, which had by this point become rambling, separate stories about each particular character, into one text that clarifies an overall plot that includes all the known Arthurian figures. This last flowering of Arthurian legend in the literature of the Middle Ages was written in English in the late 1460s and published as a book by William Caxton in 1485.

Malory begins his text with the miraculous birth of Arthur, fruit of the adulterous union of the warlike Uther Pendragon and the chaste Igrayne. This is closely followed by the other important aspects of Arthur's early career: his coronation, his acquisition of the sword Excaleber from the Lady of the Lake, and his incestuous coupling with his sister Morgawse. Arthur attempts to cover this last mistake by ruthlessly drowning all the babies born around the same time (cf. Matthew 2:16). This brutality earns for Arthur the hatred of many powerful families, but does not kill the infant Mordred.

For some time Arthur escapes the repercussions of his guilt, as he wages triumphant campaigns against the Romans and the Saracens. By aiding her father, Lodegraunce, Arthur wins the fair Gwenyvere, who brings Uther's Round Table as her dowry. Arthur surrounds the table with knights of unmatched prowess, like Launcelot, Trystrame, and Galahad, who fight to remove evil from the world. All goes well for some time until the early seeds blossom into evil.

The final disintegration of the once-indomitable Order of the Round Table is caused, in the *Morte*, by many factors: Launcelot is Arthur's greatest knight and best friend, but he loves the King's wife, just as Trystrame loves La Beale Isode, wife of King Mark. The sainted Galahad is conceived when Launcelot is tricked into unfaithfulness to the Queen by Elayne; the bastard child becomes a knight so pure that the Holy Grail (the vessel used at the Last Supper and later to collect the blood of Christ as He hung on the cross) again visits earth because of Galahad's presence; thus begins a quest from which most of the knights do not return. Simultaneously, Aggravayne and Gawayne succeed in a plot to trap Launcelot and Gwenyvere together. When the knight arrives to save his lady, he accidentally kills the brothers of Aggravayne and Gawayne. Gawayne demands vengeance from Arthur, his uncle, so they leave to wage war on Launcelot across the sea. While Arthur is away, Mordred seizes the kingdom and the Queen. Arthur returns to reprimand Mordred in a battle that begins through a mere accident when a soldier steps on a snake. This war leaves only Arthur, Mordred, and Bedyvere standing.

Arthur kills Mordred, receives a mortal wound, and is taken away in a barge by mourning women in black hoods. Bedyvere returns Excaleber to the lake and laments his lonely position.[1] Gwenyvere dies soon after as an abbess in the nunnery of Almysburye, and Launcelot, another newcomer to the monastic life, also soon dies.

Malory greatly simplifies the form for his English audience, dropping most of the magic and religious mysteries, while adding realism. His method is a swift presentation of action that avoids complicated emotional analysis. Whereas Chrétien excelled at psychological passages illuminating the inner life of a character, Malory relies upon showing rather than telling. Many times there is a message, but it is rarely direct; one must decipher the carefully contrived layering of scenes. In the *Morte*, the characters are not interested in word puns, and there is much more direct conversation with few narrative interventions, so the dialogue must be assessed by the reader (LaFarge 227).

Malory does not tantalize, but seems intent on clarifying the events for himself and his readers (Vinaver 1545). The work can be viewed as composed of eight sections. The first two concentrate on Arthur's rise to power; the next three show him at his height; the final three concentrate on the downfall of Camelot. This configuration, according to D. S. Brewer, "makes sense in itself because it describes a general chronological progression, just like life, and is also comprehensible to medieval views of life. Growth, flowering and decay; rise, supremacy and fall not only completely accord with normal experience, but can easily be imagined in such medieval terms as Fortune's wheel" (241).

Malory's work, with its frequent contradictions in detail and often confusing arrangement, is by no means perfect. But the story retains its beauty and dissolution, and most of Malory's embroidery is an improvement. Much of what Malory discarded from French writers involved Merlin and Morgan le Fay, as the author is clearly concerned with the political ramifications of Arthur's decisions; possibly this interest in battle rather than magic, and especially the civil strife that ends Arthur's kingdom, reflects Malory's perception of the Wars of the Roses (1455-85), which were ravaging England as he wrote. Malory was a knight himself, but apparently one not interested in outmoded concepts of courtly love; possibly for this reason he eliminated many of the love scenes between Launcelot and Gwenyvere, while concentrating on Launcelot as a Christian warrior. Chrétien's *Lancelot* portrays this knight as the Queen's willing pawn who is often made to look foolish for his love. Malory removed from Launcelot's character most aspects of the fawning courtly lover and substituted a warrior of great courage. Malory also increased Arthur's knightly prowess.

Arthur was not merely an English king, but a British one, so his name was used as a political tool by the Welsh Tudors from the ascension of Henry VII in 1485, the same year in which Caxton published the *Morte*.[2] Caxton's preface claims Arthur's historicity as "the moost renomed Crysten kyng . . . whyche ought moost to be remembred emonge us Englysshemen tofore al other Crysten kynges" (cxliii), but the evidence was too flimsy; the Tudors eventually chose Alfred the Great for their hero because his existence was indisputable and most of his actions had been carefully documented.

There are many theories suggesting different kings whom Malory may have intended Arthur to reflect. William Matthews believes that Malory wrote against Edward III, "whose military successes, like Arthur's, had brought him within reach of the emperor's crown, but whose ambition combined with ill luck had resulted in senseless and profitless campaigns which had made him widely unpopular" (188). R. M. Lumiansky finds in the work a sympathy for Edward IV ("Sir Thomas" 882), while *The Arthurian Encyclopedia* (1986) notes that a passage near the end of *Morte* suggests that Malory sympathized with the ousted Lancastrian King Henry VI (Lacy 352).

By far the most comprehensive argument for the work as a parallel to other military triumphs and disasters is Eugène Vinaver's discussion of the idealized portrait of Arthur as a tribute to Henry V. Malory alters the section about Arthur and Emperor Lucius to make Arthur's expedition against the Romans resemble Henry V's triumphant campaign in France. Both kings follow the same route, appoint two leaders to rule while they are away, and are called rulers of two kingdoms. "Whether as a Lancastrian or as a follower of Warwick who had sworn allegiance to Henry VI while fighting his advisers and even resisted the Duke of York's attempt to assume the crown, Malory had every reason to remember Henry V as the model of the crowned knight!" (Vinaver xxxii).

D. S. Brewer agrees with Vinaver that Malory's work may be a tribute to Henry V, but adds that it is more likely a tribute to Arthur himself and all that he stood for in the author's imagination. Brewer suggests that Malory postponed Arthur's fall so that the king can become established in greatness (239). It would seem likely also that Malory added this postponement, which allowed Arthur to be crowned Emperor of Rome and rise to further glory, to elevate the tragedy, making the ultimate fall greater.

Malory's devotion to the chivalric past is evident, and he expresses scorn for the system's disintegration because "the people were soo new fangill" (1229; bk. 21, chap. 1). This is especially touching when we recall that Malory wrote in an age of great change, "when the art of printing, the new learning and the reformation were soon to sweep away all outgrowths of chivalric romance and devoted naive, primitive faith and religion" (Ven-Ten Bensel 154). There seems to have been a fifteenth-century reversion to the Middle Ages in several important, but mostly negative, aspects that Malory may have resented: "the Lollard heresy was repressed, the real authority of Parliament declined, the Wars of the Roses restored the anarchy of feudalism" (MacCallum 89).

Malory's books of "The Tale of the Sank Greal" rely upon the French Vulgate Quest for the outline of story of the Holy Grail; Malory did little to alter the basic material, but again his skill is shown in omitting selected expositions on the doctrines of grace and salvation. In the French version, a multitude of hermits sermonize to various questing knights. Malory diminishes the distinction between religious and secular chivalry, making the distance less apparent between saintly Galahad and his more earthly father, Launcelot. The result is not always sound theology, but it does serve to integrate the Grail Quest, a part of the work that had always seemed separate from the rest of the legend because of its intense moralizing.

Malory's conclusion, the aftermath of the battle between Arthur and Mordred, seems the most brilliant and majestic part of the *Morte*. Whereas violence and magic dominate early Arthurian tales, Malory's work is more concerned with feudal laws of loyalty and setting forth a more coherent definition of chivalry:

> At his greatest, in the final passages dealing with the last battle and death of Arthur, he seems to reflect in an enlarged form all the troubles of his own society, the ruin which civil strife had brought upon him and his kind. This is imaginatively seen in the dissolution of the Table Round, the bond and fellowship of knighthood. Conquest, like true and faithful love, belongs to the past: the first and last campaigns of Arthur represent for Malory a youthful hope of the past contrasted with a tragic present. (Bradbrook 395-96)

Without gratuitous moralizing, Malory expanded the nobility of Arthur and the enduring love of Launcelot and Gwenyvere for each other and the king; this devotion restores the story's unrelenting tragedy and adds a climax of befitting grandeur never before attained. The entire tale becomes a grim vision with relevance to any civilization as Malory explores the forces, both internal and external, that ruin a kingdom.

While Launcelot does feel contrition for his sins when he confesses to a priest that he has "loved a quene unmesurabely and oute of mesure longe" (897; bk. 13, chap. 20),[3] Malory does not blame this love, nor the love of Trystrame and Isode, for the fall. Caxton asserts in his preface that Malory's work is moral in tone because it teaches readers "the noble actes of chyvalrye, the jentyl and vertuous dedes that somme knyghtes used in tho dayes, by whyche they came to honour, and how they that were vycious were punysshed and ofte put to shame and rebuke" (qtd. in Vinaver cxlv). The consensus among critics, however, is that Malory's work is not intended to be didactic. Many note that the fall seems caused by conflicting loyalties: Launcelot owes allegiance to Arthur, but loves Gwenyvere (Zesmer 109); Arthur admires Launcelot, but his ties of kinship with Gawayne are stronger (Harrington 66); and as Arthur's illegitimate and unacknowledged son, Mordred feels that he owes the King no special loyalty (Kindrick 65).

This concern with loyalty seems explainable as a key aspect of chivalry. Most of the knights become disloyal because of their great ambitions, especially in the quest for the Grail and the backing of Mordred. It is understandable that the knights are untrue to Arthur and the chivalric code: "since they cannot understand the meaning and purpose of the King's ideals, his followers fail to keep the vows of the high order of knighthood" (Ven-Ten Bensel 154). Beyond virtue, true chivalry depends upon blind obedience and loyalty to a cause, a rule of conduct that establishes order in times of disorder (Vinaver xxxiii). It is in times of struggle that chivalry is tested, and, as Malory clearly shows (possibly despite himself), it does not always work. Most of the knights are neither virtuous nor unambitious enough to follow the strict code. The Round Table fellowship fails, "and this was the fate of chivalry, because as a guiding principle, it was unequal to the problem which it undertook, and men soon saw that it merely professed to give the answer" (MacCallum 95-96). Arthur may have had the best of intentions, but he was surrounded by ordinary men of lesser standards. This is one of the main problems addressed in Tennyson's *Idylls of the King*.

Malory's work was followed by an almost total eclipse of interest in the legends, which were nearly forgotten until the latter half of the eighteenth century. Arthur rarely appears in the intervening period when advocates of classical learning and of the Reformation were alike hostile to the medieval splendors of Arthur's court. Wisely, many historians of Tudor England questioned the truth of Geoffrey of Monmouth's chronicle; therefore, many historians of the period deleted Arthur's name.

Arthur as prince is a central figure of Edmund Spenser's *Faerie Queene* (1590-96), but this is invented material about the blank period in the character's life from his birth to his accession to the throne. The name is traditional, but the character is not the same.

Between 1639 and 1641, Milton considered writing an Arthurian epic, but decided instead to write *Paradise Lost* (1667). In 1684, John Dryden wrote the libretto for the composer Henry Purcell's *King Arthur*, which was not performed until 1691. This work is not actually about Arthurian legend and uses Arthur only as a symbol of chivalry and kingship.

With the Gothic Revival and the Romantics came some interest in the Arthurian cycle. In 1813, Sir Walter Scott published "The Bridal of Triermain," an Arthurian poem. William Wordsworth's "The Egyptian Maid" (1835) refers to Sir Galahad, although here he is married, while all previous Grail stories refer to Galahad as the "virgin knight." There were, of course, during these two centuries, other stories of Arthurian characters, but none of great significance until Alfred Tennyson published his first Arthurian poem in 1832.

NOTES

1. Bedyvere's mourning is in the *ubi sunt* tradition of Old English works such as *The Wanderer* and *The Seafarer*. Bedyvere laments, for example, "A, my lorde Arthur, what shal becom of me, now ye go frome me and leve me here alone amonge myne enemyes?" (1240; bk. 21, chap. 5).

2. Henry VII shrewdly named his heir Arthur (Simmons 25).

3. August J. App condemns Malory for this "last minute attempt to 'whitewash' Lancelot clean of the sinful love for Guinevere and from the consequences of it . . . . [This] is also the one crime that bars Malory's Lancelot from being the truly grand, tragic, sinful yet admirable, character that he might be" (85).

Chapter 2

Alfred Tennyson

The popularization of the Arthurian legends in the nineteenth century can be credited mostly to Alfred Tennyson's versions of them. Malory's vast *Le Morte Darthur* with its archaic language and style of narration was too daunting for most readers; far more accessible was Tennyson's abridged and reworked version in *Idylls of the King*, which was first published in its entirety in 1891. Tennyson began giving his readership parts of his more palatable, Victorianized edition as early as 1832 with "The Lady of Shalott."

Tennyson's work on Arthurian subjects progressed steadily for the next sixty years: after the death of his friend Arthur H. Hallam, he wrote "Morte d'Arthur" in 1833-34. This poem was subsequently incorporated into "The Passing of Arthur," the last of the *Idylls*. "Merlin and Vivien" was written in 1855-56, followed by "Enid" and "Enid and Geraint." The first four Idylls were published in 1859 as "Enid," "Vivien," "Elaine," and "Guinevere," and these became about one-half of the finished version. In 1869 Tennyson published "The Coming of Arthur," "The Holy Grail," "Palleas and Ettarre," and "The Passing of Arthur." In 1871 "The Last Tournament" was published and later reprinted with "Gareth and Lynette" in 1872. "Balin and Balan" was written in 1872-74, but was not published until 1885. public response was enormous, sequence was not printed together until 1891.

Tennyson's reworking of Malory shows an important shift in moral emphasis. Malory allows many factors to dissolve Arthur's court, especially the knights' departure on the Grail Quest, but

Tennyson's parallel account emphasizes a single moral failure, the sin of Lancelot and Guinevere, a love Malory did not condemn. For contemporary critics such as Thomas Carlyle, George Meredith, and Algernon Swinburne, such reworkings failed to enhance the legends; still, these poems were popular with a public hungry for works about the Middle Ages. However, those who had read Malory generally preferred his more robust and passionate story (Martin 424).

Victorian criticism of the *Idylls* varied extremely: aesthetes saw beautiful pictures marred by moral significance while more puritanical critics disapproved of the indulgence in the senses and wanted a more austere moral lesson. In *King Arthur's Laureate* (1971), J. Philip Eggers finds this dichotomy to be "a symptom of the very failure that Camelot presents, the alienation of beauty from social purpose, or, figuratively, the failure to make culture prevail" (68-69). Thomas Carlyle charged that Tennyson was hiding behind "a medieval arras" to avoid "the horror of the Industrial Revolution" (qtd. in Priestley 35); these, as well as John Sterling's *Quarterly* review that the "miraculous legend of 'Excalibur' . . . reproduced by any modern gentleman must be a mere ingenious exercise of fancy" (Gilbert 864), reflect a lack of comprehension of Tennyson's goal. Admittedly, it is true that his intentions are not always identifiable, and often seem purposefully ambiguous. This indicates Tennyson's "extraordinarily explicit honesty, so that at the moment we expect affirmation he affirms, but at the same time he confesses that he is not so sure as the words might sound" because he writes about the "tension between powerful and unresolvable opposites" (Smith 195).

Beyond beautiful lyric poetry and individual parables, the *Idylls* do seem to convey several meanings, some of them contrasting, of importance to Victorian society. From a comprehensive view, the work is about the decline of a community from an original, ideal state. Most of the corruption is caused by human sexuality, particularly female passion--a topic that had gained in contemporary importance with all the attention to the question of a woman's rightful role in society (Hellstrom 109). The *Idylls* can also be seen as an outcry against modern life, or "wasted civilization" (Burchell 424), a work that mirrors contemporary problems caused by the juxtaposition of Victorian self-confidence with the equally powerful Victorian deep despair: the feeling that this was a golden, ideal time was undercut by the knowledge that it could suddenly end. The age was complex and paradoxical, sometimes optimistic and sometimes melancholy, and Tennyson's *Idylls* reflects this perfectly.

Tennyson follows Malory closely in plot, but the Victorian poet's additions and omissions significantly change the import of the story. Although Tennyson's "indebtedness is at first sight very great" and such comparisons have often led to his being described as "a copyist, and even a bad copyist," he alters the legends to speak to his era (MacCallum 96). It would seem wise for critics to discontinue the habit of judging Arthurian legend in terms of any good/bad hierarchy, a rating system that often disparages Tennyson's text. While he did lessen the vividness and earthiness of his predecessors' story, Tennyson created a work palatable to Victorian audiences.

The charge that he clothed Victorian characters in medieval costumes (Hughes, "Urban" 43) is correct; Tennyson brings the subject to the Victorian public and does not expect readers to be historians or scholars able to easily understand an earlier time. Instead, the author creates what has been called "ethical medievalism" (Mancoff 19), conceptions of legendary characters who could be emulated in everyday life, rather than presenting lovers as a subsidiary interest whose fate was shaped by issues of war, governance or the chivalric code. Tennyson's approach was both pluralistic and domestic, centering on individuals and localized narratives more than on issues of national identity and fate (Hughes, "Urban" 43).

Certainly, the characters are highly individualized and fascinating (with the possible exception of Arthur), but because few of the interpersonal relationships end well, the *Idylls* is a depressing story of decay and ruin. To clarify the correlation between Tennyson's message and the fate of each important character in terms of love and death, each profile will be commented upon separately.

ARTHUR

The king is a gentle, modest man who rages only on the battlefield, where he relies upon the fire of God. Whereas the Arthur of Sir Thomas Malory sins by committing incest with Morgawse and is shamed (as well as ultimately murdered by the fruit of that union), Tennyson's Arthur is blameless and reports honestly to Guinevere, "I was ever virgin save for thee" ("Guinevere" 554). His fault is his subconscious moral superiority: blind to the baseness of others, he assumes that they are equally pure. A love of human beings that is completely trusting makes Tennyson's Arthur frequently seem Christlike, a connection the author strengthens with scenes that parallel biblical passages.[1] This has prompted many critics to note that Arthur is not powerful enough as a man and seems a "mere absence of vice; the allegorical and the literal simply do not enforce each other" (Martin 495). Since the poem "Morte d'Arthur" was written in grief at Tennyson's friend Arthur Hallam's death,[2] some theorize that the "Christ/King Arthur/Arthur Hallam" figure shows the poet attempting to establish "a possible significance for his friend's life and death" (Hunt, "Poetry"117). Robert Bernard Martin (1980) finds that the poet's inadequate characterization of King Arthur stems from Tennyson's having known the model too well and being unable to realize that he had failed to render his vision on paper (495). However,

Arthur, a remote mythological figure of superhuman ethics, is difficult to interpret. He is able to establish a new moral code that holds allegiance and faith supreme. This occurs, in part, because Arthur's ideals are partially reflected in the oath of the Round Table:

> To reverence the King, as if he were
> Their conscience, and their conscience as their king,
> To break the heathen and uphold the Christ,
> To ride abroad redressing human wrongs.
> To speak no slander, no, nor listen to it,
> To honour his own word as if his Gods,
> To lead sweet lives in purest chastity,
> To love one maiden only, cleave to her,
> And worship her by years of noble deeds,
> Until they won her.
>
> ("Guinevere" 465-74)

Although this oath seems to indicate the same tentative connection seen in medieval writing between Christianity and courtly love, Tennyson's Arthur does not intend that the maiden so faithfully served should be the knight's mistress. He never imagines Lancelot and Guinevere's relationship, except for one brief moment of suspicion when both lovers announce that they will not attend the diamond joust ("Lancelot and Elaine" 127).

The majority of the court at Camelot knows of Guinevere's adultery, but Arthur remains blissfully unaware; apparently, the king trusts that his queen loves him and does not imagine that she could commit such a sin. Throughout the *Idylls* Tennyson uses an appearance-versus-reality motif; Guinevere's deception is the most devastating example. When Arthur, newly crowned king, falls in love with her at her father Leodogran's castle at Cameliard, it is solely on the basis of her physical beauty. Arthur rides off to do his duty in battle after he has seen, but not spoken to her. Immediately upon his return, Arthur asks Leodogran for Guinevere's hand, assuming that her attractive facade indicates spiritual beauty.

Leodogran lingers over the decision to pledge his only child, not because he desires to know Guinevere's feelings, she was so unimpressed with Arthur that she failed to notice him among the other soldiers, but because he worries about Arthur's questionable parentage. Inasmuch as Tennyson does not attempt to make Arthur's heritage definite, this is one of many instances when the poet makes his hero seem more a mythical than historical figure.[3] Bellicent and Bedivere are unable to clarify details of Arthur's birth, but what ultimately persuades Leodogran to concede is a dream he has of a "phantom" king crowned in heaven.

Although Arthur's position is not proven to be inherited, he does have an interior energy that Elliot L. Gilbert sees as a creative ahistorical type of a distinctly female nature (865).[4] Indeed, most readers of the *Idylls* wonder how the traditionally virile and manly Arthur of legend and romance evolved into Tennyson's restrained monarch. It is Arthur's passionless, benign nature that allows Tennyson's Camelot to flourish at first as an ennobling place, one where women are welcomed, protected, and given great freedom. It is this enormous liberty and trust that causes the tragic outcome; as the model of human perfection, Arthur does not realize what is happening around him and does not bother to question the situation, created by his own spouse, until he is forced to recognize this evil. Arthur's brand of removed and impractical heroism reminds one of the problems Tennyson addressed in "The Lotos-Eaters," "The Palace of Art," and to a lesser extent in "The Lady of Shalott": is it a good idea for a creative force that is content in seclusion to mingle with normal human beings? Many times Arthur would have had the power to thwart destructive personalities within the kingdom had he only been aware of their intentions; he was, rather, blinded by an almost absurd utopian optimism that makes him a poor leader because it allows him to be broken by the rudeness of the real world. Guinevere speaks truly when she says of her husband, "He is all fault who hath no fault at all" ("Lancelot and Elaine" 132).

Arthur is not wrong in what he desires to accomplish, only in believing that he can mold the normal individuals around him into something greater than they are in actuality. When Arthur first arrives, the land is dominated by beasts; these he promptly expels along with the "heathens." This Christian king may realize that "more things are wrought by prayer, / Than this world dreams of" ("The Passing of Arthur" 415-16), but his followers are incapable of the same faith. Tennyson makes the other characters seem more like the animals that were removed from the land than like their leader, perhaps indicating that Arthur tried to push the evolutionary process of men who were unready for civilization (Eggers 195).[5] Human beings need the guidance of a metaphysical ideal, but it must be an ethic they can understand and one that is enforced; Tennyson's Arthur has a bit of charisma, which gains attention at first, but he does not have the firm grasp of a dictator. Camelot as utopia is an illusion, because no community is completely static and Arthur does not have enough knowledge of human nature to expect the inevitable downward progression from an original, ideal state. There is a moment before his final undoing when Arthur has a feeling that his men are not as loyal as he expects them to be, and he complains to Lancelot of his annoyance:

> The foot that loiters, bidden go,--the glance
> That only seems half-loyal to command,--
> A manner somewhat fall'n from reverence
> Or have I dream'd the bearing of our knights
> Tells of a manhood ever less and lower?
>   ("The Last Tournament" 117-21)

The knights do not fully respect their leader because they know about the Queen's indiscretion and because they are annoyed by the King's blindness or lack of concern. When Arthur discovers the extent of his wife's unfaithfulness, he behaves in a typically unmasculine way by remaining calm, dignified, and merciful. Malory's Arthur does not become furious either, but this is because he had some warning that his wife was more than just an inspiration to his best friend. Practically, Malory's Arthur is more upset about losing the Round Table fellowship than about losing Gwenyvere:

> "And therefore," seyde the kynge, ""wyte you well, my harte was never so hevy as hit ys now. And much more I am soryar for my knyghtes losse than for the losse of my fayre quene; for quenys I myght have inow, but such a felyship of good knyghtes shall never be togydirs in no company."
> (1183-84; bk. 20, chap. 9)

Tennyson's king is much more concerned with his queen, especially with educating her about exactly what she has done wrong. First, however, he strikes a cruel blow when he says to her, "Well it is that no child is born of thee" ("Guinevere" 421), a comment that seems rather more a pragmatic concern than an indication of the shame Guinevere should be feeling. After he tells her that he will surely meet his doom soon after he leaves the nunnery, Arthur adds his most cutting remark: "Thou hast not made my life so sweet to me, / That I the King should greatly care to live; / For thou hast spoilt the purpose of my life" ("Guinevere" 448-50).

Arthur becomes more compassionate later in this long speech, but ever more priggish: "I did not come to curse thee, Guinevere, / I, whose vast pity almost makes me die / . . . Lo! I forgive thee, as Eternal God / Forgives" ("Guinevere" 530-31, 541-42). Although he claims to give her absolution in his heart, Arthur, the man of spirit, cannot touch her hand because "that too is flesh,/ And in the flesh thou hast sinn'd" ("Guinevere" 550-51). However, he does tell her twice after this that he loves her still and that his last hope is to be reclaimed as her husband in heaven. After he has made the sign of the cross over her head, Arthur leaves Guinevere groveling on the chamber floor.

Arthur's reaction to the Queen's deception seems rather cool, but a reader is unlikely to be shocked, having never been convinced that he cared for her beyond her incomparable beauty. Had he paid her more attention, Arthur could have discovered that Guinevere did not have the spirituality he expected to accompany her looks. Arthur did not probe beyond the surface, but simply trusted that she was devoted. Since the King is Tennyson's hero, we must believe that the poet meant for Arthur's good faith to symbolize the pinnacle of married love-trust in the mate's purity--rather than some type of self-delusion.

In the same removed kingly manner, Arthur rides out to meet his death at the hand of Modred. The images of destruction are overwhelming as the armies clash "on the waste sand by the waste sea" ("The Passing of Arthur" 93). At the end of the nightmarish battle, only Arthur, Modred, and Bedivere are left alive, and Arthur begins to doubt, "for on my heart hath fallen / Confusion, till I know not what I am, / Nor whence I am, nor whether I be king; / Behold, I seem but King among the dead" ("The Passing of Arthur" 143-46).

Pointing to Modred, who is the only member of the opposition still standing, Bedivere calls him the "traitor of thine house," to which Arthur answers, "My house hath been my doom" ("The Passing of Arthur" 153, 154). This last statement of blame is true, especially if Arthur is thinking of Guinevere. Uncle and nephew give each other parting blows, actions that are relayed in a language far less graphic than Malory's,[6] and Arthur is soon carried away in a barge bound for Avilion because "From the great deep to the great deep he goes" ("The Passing of Arthur" 445).

Arthur's death is somewhat bleaker in the *Morte* than in the *Idylls* because Malory includes a possible gravesite for the King's body after the dying Arthur departs with the mourning queens. Both works include the messianic idea that the king will return when his people need him most. Tennyson concludes on a hopeful note, with Bedivere glimpsing the sunlight of a new year and faintly hearing a cheering city welcoming Arthur. Malory continues with his fatalistic view by including Launcelot and Gwenyvere's dismal last meeting scene and separate deaths. Tennyson does not allow his audience to witness the lovers' final periods of repentance or their eventual salvation.

Tennyson's Arthur, the idealistic statesman, always seems more symbol than man. Since his entire life is reflected in the changing seasons, we expect him to die with the old year and feel little sorrow for him as a character; we do, however, feel immense distress for the death of his ideal. Arthur's failure is more than simply the end of Camelot; it symbolizes the triumph of evil in the souls of human beings. Arthur seems an unfortunate ruler because he trusted and was trustworthy in a world unfit for a champion of his caliber. His reign and death are the inevitable end of such a pure dream.

GUINEVERE

In most medieval English literature, genealogy and kinship are discussed in terms of men. Members of a patrilineal society, females become secondary, even when they belong to wealthy or royal families. Women are often used as "Peace-weavers" ("freoð-webbe" in *Beowulf*, line 1943) who bind powerful, sometimes feuding, clans by marrying into another group and producing sons. Although the practice of a parent choosing a daughter's spouse had eroded somewhat by the Victorian era, Tennyson--even though his characters are thoroughly Victorian--continues the tradition. When King Leodogran allows his only child to be wedded to Arthur, a ruler whose heritage is uncertain, it is the greatest act of faith he can make as well as a reflection of his appreciation of the help rendered him by the younger, stronger man. Guinevere's feelings are not considered in this masculine pact.

Although at the marriage ceremony Guinevere replies demurely to Arthur's profession of endless love, "King and my lord, I love thee to the death!" ("The Coming of Arthur" 469), Tennyson gives the reader little news of the Queen until later when she has become a malevolent force. In the third of the twelve idylls, "The Marriage of Geraint," Guinevere is already suspect:

> But when a rumour rose about the Queen,
> Touching her guilty love for Lancelot,
> Tho' yet there lived no proof, nor yet was heard
> The world's loud whisper breaking into storm,

Not less Geraint believed it.

(24-28)

The Queen has probably broken her wedding vow even at this early stage, and if we believe that one of the cohesive purposes of the *Idylls* is an exploration of love relationships, we must wonder why Tennyson has Guinevere become unfaithful so prematurely. (Malory does not suggest this possibility until much later.) The climate of Victorian England was still largely one of male dominion, and contemporary reviewers overwhelmingly blamed Guinevere rather than Arthur or Lancelot (Eggers 87-89); still, it may not be true that this type of reading was totally Tennyson's intention. Certainly the poet does not advocate wives cuckolding their husbands, but he does make a sustained effort to show that Arthur and Guinevere are of entirely different natures. Arthur's decision to make Guinevere his queen is one based upon a glance at her as he rides off to battle, possibly illustrating the adage "marry in haste, repent in long leisure."

If it is true that "the woman question is more or less central to all the books of 'The Round Table' . . . and perhaps the most significant and revolutionary question of the ninteenth century" (Hellstrom 109), Guinevere's position as the female character of highest potential must make her downfall simply something beyond the obvious. There is ample evidence that Tennyson, in other aspects of the *Idylls,* purposefully depicted the corrosive nature of human sexuality, especially female passion. Because the Queen is neither ambitious nor vicious like Ettarre and Vivien, we are forced to read her motivation differently from the motivations of these other two destructive women.

Before Guinevere sees Arthur--since she did not note his presence among other knights at her father's castle--she meets the dashing, handsome Lancelot, who is sent to accompany her to the King. Uncertain at the very least and likely very frightened, Guinevere unsurprisingly forms a lasting bond with Lancelot; he becomes her protector, an association strengthened by his constant supreme prowess in knightly endeavors. Since Lancelot and Arthur "swear on the field of death a deathless love" ("The Coming of Arthur" 131) and are constant companions, it stands to reason that Guinevere compares the two. She remembers her first sight of the king: she "glanced at him, thought him cold, / High, self-contained, and passionless, not like him, / Not like my Lancelot" ("Guinevere" 402-04). Later, she describes the differences between the two to Lancelot:

> Arthur, my lord, Arthur, the faultless king,
> That passionate perfection, my good lord--
> But who can gaze upon the sun in heaven?
> He never spake word of reproach to me,
> He never had a glimpse of mine untruth,
> He cares not for me: only here to-day
> There gleam'd a vague suspicion in his eyes:
> Some meddling rogue has tamper'd with him--else
> Rapt in this fancy of his Table Round,
> And swearing men to vows impossible,
> To make them like himself: but, friend, to me
> He is all fault who hath no fault at all:
> For who loves me must have a touch of earth;
> The low sun makes the colour: I am yours,
> Not Arthur's, as ye know, save by the bond.
>   ("Lancelot and Elaine" 121-35)

Guinevere needs "earth" and "colour" to sustain her love, a reflection of her sensuous nature. She is not the spiritual creature Arthur desired as a mate.

Perhaps Guinevere turns to Lancelot to protest her position as a pawn, and this may also explain why she produces no heir for Arthur (although we cannot clearly imagine Arthur engaging in any pastime so earthy as copulation). The King and Queen have a relationship of sterility produced by opposing values; even the baby Arthur discovers abandoned quickly dies when placed in Guinevere's care. It seems that Guinevere takes her revenge for her unhappiness with the king whenever opportunities present themselves.

Today, it is not especially hard to feel great sympathy for Guinevere's rebellion against oppression or to understand her desire for escapism; however, perhaps because of a long-standing tradition of realizing the opposite position, critics rarely show any compassion for the Queen and likewise do not find Tennyson encouraging such sensibility. Still, as Guinevere grovels face down on the nunnery floor in her last scene, suddenly conscious of the havoc she has wreaked and choked by Arthur's mercy, only a very cold heart would not pity her. Perhaps the critics and readers who remain unmoved are taken by the momentum of Arthur's powerful monologue, particularly his list of her crimes:

> Then came thy shameful sin with Lancelot;
> Then came the sin of Tristram and Isolt;
> Then others, following these my mightiest knights,
> And drawing foul ensample from fair names,
> Sinn'd also, till the loathsome opposite
> Of all my heart had destined did obtain,
> And all thro' thee.
>
> ("Guinevere" 484-90)

Further, after Arthur departs to fight Modred, Guinevere speaks to herself of her guilt in terms that would make a sympathetic reader feel like a dolt:

> Shall I kill myself?
> What help in that? I cannot kill my sin,
> If soul be soul; nor can I kill my shame;
> No, nor by living can I live it down.
> The days will grow to weeks, the weeks to months,
> The months will add themselves and make the years,
> The years will roll into the centuries,
> And mine will ever be the name of scorn.
>
> ("Guinevere" 615-22)

Evidently the punishment for ignoring an unwanted husband and social responsibility is an abominable reputation that lingers in the minds of somewhat unthoughtful readers forever.

As in the *Morte*, the Guinevere of the *Idylls* dies as the nunnery's abbess and finds peace in the hereafter. There is, however, a vast difference between the two writers' reasons for granting Guinevere a tranquil eternal rest. In the *Morte* the Queen is judged in terms of her adherence to the doctrine of courtly love: "whyle she lyved she was a trew lover, and therfor she had a good ende" (1120;

bk. 18, chap. 25). Tennyson takes the opposite stance: since Guinevere repents deeply for having been Lancelot's mistress and does her penance at length while living in the nunnery, she finds peace. There is, as well, the pleasant possibility offered by Tennyson's Arthur that Guinevere may reclaim her husband--if she so desires--in heaven, after her soul has been cleansed. It would seem that the opportunity to make exactly this decision on her own was all Guinevere truly desired from the outset.

LANCELOT

Tennyson's Lancelot has little in common with Malory's high-spirited, stylish hero of the same name (spelled "Launcelot"). The *Idylls* focuses on the catastrophic consequences of adultery, so Lancelot's role is shameful rather than glamorous. By omitting all of this knight's scenes of gallantry that are central to the early legends--such as the occasions when he dashingly saves his lover from immediate death--Tennyson changes the essence of the Lancelot/Guinevere love story to a warning against such behavior. Malory's Launcelot is to be admired and emulated; further, to avoid any possible offence, Malory adds the possibility that the connection between the Queen and her knight was not of the "modern" type and may have been purely platonic and virtuous:

> And ryght so faryth the love nowadayes, sone hote sone colde. Thys ys no stabylyte. But the olde love was nat so. For men and women coude love togydirs seven yerys, and no lycoures lustis was betwyxte tham, and than was love trouthe and faythefulnes. And so in lyke wyse was used such love in kynge Arthurs dayes.
>
> (1120; bk. 18, chap. 25)

Tennyson's comments upon the immoral, corrupt bond between Guinevere and Lancelot show a stance completely antagonistic to Malory's understanding and acceptance of courtly love.

Some hold the opinion that "Lancelot, like Milton's Satan, stole the show in spite of the author" (Girouard 184), a reaction likely stemming from the Victorians' overwhelming acceptance of Lancelot, while they blamed the tragedy completely on Guinevere (Eggers 89). Also, if Lancelot "steals the show," it is because he is the most clearly defined male character and seems so much more human than the king; while he is by no means the passionate, dramatic hero of the *Morte*--primarily because his love for Guinevere is passive--he does appear to be a great soul trapped and unable to delight in the forbidden desire that seems fated to destroy him. Still, passive or not, it seems only fair that Lancelot should equally share the culpability with Guinevere. Perhaps this indicates that despite the overall didactic tone of the *Idylls,* "Tennyson deliberately thwarted the Victorian tendency toward rigid moralism" (Eggers 82) by giving Lancelot some degree of beauty.

Earlier, Tennyson wrote a fragment called "Sir Launcelot and Queen Guinevere" (1842) in which the affair is not so sanitized; the lovers are portrayed sympathetically in a poem that concentrates on the joy and beauty of spring in a mood neither pejorative nor tragic. According to the poet's friend J. M. Kemnble, an unpublished earlier version of the fragment included Launcelot singing a long, romantic song as he took Guinevere to live with him at Joyous Guard after having saved her from being burned as an adulteress (Ricks 502-5). It seems likely that Tennyson removed this portion of the poem to make it appear less probable that he was condoning adultery.

Except for the garden scene that drives Balin to madness, the reader is never privy to any erotic or even tender moments between Lancelot and Guinevere. By the beginning of the seventh idyll, "Lancelot and Elaine," the Queen has grown somewhat weary of her lover's attentions and is more concerned with inhibiting rumors than with titillating her knight. However, even though "the great and guilty love he bare the Queen . . . drove him into the wastes and solitudes for agony" ("Lancelot and Elaine" 244, 251), Lancelot will not be wooed by Elaine because he feels himself bound forever to Guinevere.

When Lancelot wears Elaine's red sleeve embroidered with pearls in the diamond jousts, he does so as part of his disguise, so that he may fight unknown. Elaine, already smitten by his charm and courtesy, considers this attention a prelude to deeper intimacy, a reaction underscored when Lancelot thoughtlessly rewards her by reflecting, "I never yet have done so much for any maiden living" ("Lancelot and Elaine" 373-74). This declaration, as well as the brotherly kiss he offers at departing, begins the downward spiral of events that prove to be Elaine's undoing. Lancelot does not intend to cause the maiden such grief, and he is genuinely fond of her, as well as grateful when she later nurses his wounds. Their relationship seems a comment upon the King and Queen's similar situation: the man notices that the woman is beautiful, but makes no effort to delve below the surface to discover her true emotions. The connection, of course, ends here, because Elaine sees Lancelot and stands "Rapt on his face as if it were a God's," while Guinevere views her husband as much less supreme, as "a moral child without the craft to rule" ("Lancelot and Elaine" 354, 145).

Perhaps Guinevere's enormous unpopularity with Victorian audiences can be partially attributed to her refusal to glorify either Lancelot or Arthur. It must have been vexing to Victorian reviewers, most of whom were male and part of a male-dominated society, to confront a female character unimpressed by two of the greatest heroes of early English legend. In contrast, the idolatry felt by the lily maid of Astolat for Lancelot made her admired and praised, despite her complete insanity at the end of her life.[7] Elaine will not accept Lancelot's compromise of protection for life and half of his realm beyond the sea. Lancelot cannot offer to be her husband or paramour because of his guilty, but devoted, love for Guinevere. This loyalty goes unappreciated by the Queen, who rages at Lancelot for wearing Elaine's sleeve and flings the priceless diamonds that he has been collecting for nine years into the river. When Guinevere learns that Elaine is dead and that Lancelot did not encourage the maid to love him, she apologizes to her knight. Lancelot does not answer her, but ponders to himself the reason for her previous angry outburst:

> Jealousy in love?
> Not rather dead love's harsh heir, jealous pride?
> Queen, if I grant the jealousy as of love,
> May not your crescent fear for name and fame
> Speak, as it waxes, of a love that wanes?
> ("Lancelot and Elaine" 1386-90)

If the emotions felt by Lancelot and Guinevere were ever indicative of true love, those feelings have passed. Lancelot soon decides that the time has come for him to break his bond with the Queen because he knows that it is wrong; further, he realizes that until he severs all ties with Guinevere, those knights who admire him may choose a similar shameful path by following his example. This is exactly Tennyson's point: sin becomes even more contagious when it is discovered in someone who is greatly admired. In "The Last Tournament" there is the strong feeling that Lancelot's adultery induced Tristram's similar relationship with Isolt, as well as the poor behavior of the other knights. The tournament is a mockery of the earlier jousts because Lancelot is in charge and allows the knights to behave in slothful, deceitful manners that mirror his own guilt.

Ultimately, Tennyson's comment about love through the character of Lancelot seems to be that allowing an idolatrous passion to be of greater import than social duty spoils all. Lancelot's devotion to the Queen causes him to be greatly injured by his own kin, to lose the diamonds, to inadvertently cause the deaths of both Elaine and Gawain, and to encourage Modred's usurpation of the throne, which leads to Arthur's mortal wound. Clearly, these horrible results outweigh the pleasure, especially since Lancelot frequently suffers depression because of his guilt and shame. Unlike Malory, Tennyson does not allow the reader to witness Lancelot's five years of repentance and sorrow. The two lines about the knight's good end, "So groan'd Sir Lancelot in a remorseful pain, / Not knowing he should die a holy man" ("Lancelot and Elaine" 417-18), appear to be purposefully brief; it seems, as it did with Guinevere, that Tennyson did not want to encourage the idea that sinners may find salvation later, but was more concerned with discouraging any wicked conduct by concentrating on its earthly consequences.

ELAINE

Although Elaine, the lily maid of Astolat, appears only in the seventh idyll, and her character is borrowed almost entirely from Malory, she is significant for several reasons. The first, of course, is her relation to her predecessor in Tennyson's "The Lady of Shalott"

(1832). Both characters begin high in a tower, but while the Lady of Shalott soon sees Lancelot in her mirror and then through the window, Elaine has already met the knight and is carefully guarding his shield. When we meet Elaine, she has finished embroidering a case for Lancelot's shield that is an exact copy of the original, "an involved and, if we think about it, ludicrous multiplication of image upon image" (Smith 17). The idyll begins *in medias res* with Elaine indulging in fantasy reading "the events of Lancelot's career in the naked shield, again a curious and erotic scene of vicarious experience behind a barred door" (Hunt, "Poetry" 96). Thus when we meet Elaine, she has survived the events that destroyed her predecessor.

In "The Lady of Shalott," the weaver dies because a curse falls upon her for deviating from her status as an artist in seclusion; "a human being in need of human interests and affection, the artist is impelled to abandon isolation, but ironically the 'world' brings a loss of love, tragedy and death" (R. Simpson 200). She purposely renounces her ascetic life because she is "half sick of shadows" (l. 71) so she must make retribution. In the *Idylls*, Elaine's case is not so simple. As a counterpart of Arthur (Hughes "All that Makes a Man" 59; Eggers 147-48; Rosenberg *Fall* 101), Elaine is similarly unable to realize that her dream is unattainable. The supernatural elements of "The Lady of Shalott" have been removed so that in the idyll, Elaine's destruction is caused by her blind devotion to the wrong man. She lives in fantasy, a purposeful naïveté , as long as possible until her love is betrayed by reality. Although the king suggests that Lancelot's life might have been vastly improved through marriage to Elaine, Lancelot's worship of the Queen destroys that possibility from the outset. Elaine's love is unreturned, a rejection that makes her passionately desire death.[8]

Mark Girouard in *The Return to Camelot* (1981) finds Elaine--the shy, fair maid willing to die for love--to be Tennyson's ideal type of female character (198); this, however, seems unlikely if we agree that Elaine is used to underscore Arthur's problem and if we note her completely obsessive nature. When Elaine plans her elaborate death scene and forces herself to die, we must realize that she wants revenge. While it is true that Elaine could have used the letter clasped in her dead hand for much greater harm to Lancelot's reputation, she certainly does incriminate him for leaving without bidding her good-bye and for not understanding her intentions:

> I, sometime call'd the maid of Astolat,
> Come, for you left me taking no farewell,
> Hither, to take my last farewell of you.
> I loved you, and my love had no return,
> And therefore my true love has been my death,
> And therefore to our Lady Guinevere,
> And to all other ladies, I make moan:
> Pray for my soul, and yield me burial.
> ("Lancelot and Elaine" 1265-72)

Engaging in this sort of elaborate public scheme, especially after her soul's departure from this world, does not seem the sort of conduct Tennyson would encourage in a lady. Further, Elaine's earlier suggestion that she accompany Lancelot through the world without the benefit of marriage seems the bold offer of a harlot. Elaine's mania does not patently reproduce "Tennyson's ideal" at all; her unencouraged devotion to Lancelot and her induced death are the products of a disturbed mind. Elaine's obsessive nature and the twenty- year age difference between her and Lancelot validates Arthur's idea that the queen and Lancelot were well suited.

MERLIN

"Merlin and Vivien," the sixth idyll in the completed sequence, is Tennyson's version of the Samson and Delilah story in which the woman steals the man's strength (Eggers 137). Although in the *Morte* Merlin is a devil's son, Tennyson removes all of this character's association with evil as well as most of his supernatural powers. Tennyson's Merlin is still able to foretell select portions of the future, but his power is completely beneficial. Merlin is transformed into Arthur's wise advisor who does not mistakenly suggest that Arthur kill all the babies born on May Day. In the *Idylls* Merlin's only error is accepting Vivien's flattery and allowing himself to become tolerant of her ways, even though intellectually he realizes that she is insincere.

Unlike Arthur, who simply is unable to comprehend wickedness in others, Merlin understands Vivien to be a malevolent force, but underestimates the power of her physical and mental seductiveness. Merlin's abilities come from studying a book given to him by a man who rejected sensuality to concentrate on the text, which had been passed down to him by another man. This male power bequeathed through a text of charms and information does not warn of the possibility that a woman may have special powers of her own. Merlin is the only male character who "is not a warrior-knight-lover . . . but mage and bard of Arthur's realm . . . [so] the lesson is that a wise man must acquire wisdom not only in science and art but also in the ways of the flesh--particularly the ways of women--if he is to achieve and sustain his full potential" (Hughes "All that Makes a Man" 57).

Merlin's "love" for Vivien is at best a sort of apathetic forbearance of her presence. He is downcast following a premonition of his own death and does not for some time even notice the scantily clad Vivien's appearance. Because his despair has distracted him and because he knows nothing of women, Vivien is able to make Merlin disclose to her the powerful charm that creates a death-in-life situation for those it is used upon. Although Merlin does fear giving Vivien power over him through the charm, he finally trusts her posture of innocence and honesty:

> For Merlin, overtalk'd and overworn,
> Had yielded, told her all the charm and slept.
> Then, in one moment, she put forth the charm
> Of woven paces and of waving hands,
> And in the hollow oak he lay as dead,
> And lost to life and use and name and fame.
>   ("Merlin and Vivien" 963-68)

As in the story of Elaine, here, too, a love relationship directly causes immediate death; also, in both idylls, the woman is the pursuer, the man the pursued. However, Vivien does not desire Merlin as Elaine desires Lancelot; Vivien is concerned only with obtaining one piece of powerful information from the wise man so that she can use his knowledge against him in order to make herself feel superior. Tennyson makes it clear that although Vivien is wholly wicked, Merlin partially deserves eternal death-in-life for not being more discerning in his choice of companions. Merlin recognizes that Vivien is not as devoted to him as she pretends to be, but is too flattered by her attention to realize that she is especially dangerous, so he does not take the precaution of banishing her. As he allows himself to be deceived and to have his intellect corrupted by sensuality, he gets his just reward. While Malory's Arthur feels lost without Merlin, Tennyson's Arthur places his faith in God and is, therefore, better able to adjust to the wise man's disappearance.

VIVIEN

Malory's character Nenyve, the Lady of the Lake, is the source of Tennyson's Vivien; however, the later author's treatment of this femme fatale is largely original. Nenyve is not evil in the *Morte*, and although she does permanently trap Merlin in a stone, because she is provoked and frightened this is not considered wrong:

> And allwayes, he lay aboute to have hir maydynhode, and she was ever passynge wery of hym and wolde have bene delyverde of hym, for she was aferde of hym for cause he was a devyls son, and she cowde not be skyfte of him by no meane.
>
> (126; bk. 4, chap. 1)

Nenyve may have just cause, but in the *Idylls* Vivien's enchantment of Merlin stems from her desires for both revenge and fame. She tries to charm Arthur, but is ignored, so instead she entraps the king's chief advisor: "As fancying that her glory would be great / According to his greatness whom she quench'd" ("Merlin and Vivien" 215-16).

Tennyson does give the deceitful, conniving Vivien some motivation for her bold attack on Arthur and his court:

> As Love, if Love be perfect, casts out fear,
> So Hate, if Hate be perfect, casts out fear.
> My father died in a battle against the king,
> My mother on his corpse in open field;

> She bore me there, for born from death was I
> Among the dead and sown upon the wind--
> And then on thee!
>
> ("Merlin and Vivien" 40-46)

Vivien is an orphan who blames her parents' deaths on Arthur and has been aided by Mark, one of Arthur's chief foes; she is, therefore, very willing when Mark asks that she journey to Camelot to create unrest by spreading slander. Most of Vivien's rumors are intended to defame the Queen; since Guinevere kindly agrees to help the young woman she believes has been tormented and pursued by Mark, Vivien becomes one of her court ladies and is thus able to watch Guinevere closely.

Vivien, "The seeming-injured simple-hearted thing" ("Merlin and Vivien" 900), quickly schemes beyond the task she has been sent to undertake, and she determines to use her beauty and charm as tools of entrapment. Tennyson shows her contempt for morality when he has Vivien use her sexuality as a weapon for promoting her advancement. This character, like Modred, whom she later aids, has a problem that is the opposite of Arthur's: she is essentially rotten and assumes that those around her are equally wicked. With her feigned avowals of religion she also echoes the falseness of King Pellam, who pretends to accept Christianity in an excessive and narrow way in an attempt to rival the sincere devotion of his enemy, King Arthur.

Tennyson further increases a reader's awareness of Vivien's unattractiveness, despite her beautiful facade, by consistently describing her as snakelike:

> And lissome Vivien, holding by his heel,
> Writhed toward him, slided up his knee and sat,
> Behind his ankle twined her hollow feet
> Together, curved an arm about his neck,
> Clung like a snake.
>
>   . . .
>
> And hearing "harlot" mutter'd twice or thrice,
> Leapt from her session on his lap, and stood
> Stiff as a viper frozen; loathsome sight,

How from the rosy lips of life and love,
Flush'd the bare-grinning skeleton of death!
                    ("Merlin and Vivien" 236-40, 841-45)

The snake imagery and Vivien's sophistry remind one of the charming, splendidly handsome serpent of Milton's *Paradise Lost*, for both characters, subtle but fallacious reasoning combines with physical radiance to allow triumph. Tennyson does not portray Vivien's death, for her end is unimportant; what is of consequence to him is a reader's realization that this sort of false lover is to be avoided.

GERAINT

Tennyson borrowed the story of Geraint and Enid from Lady Charlotte Guest's translation of the *Mabinogion* as well as from Chrétien de Troyes's *Erec et Enide* but added much psychological insight; unlike the earlier versions that concentrate upon action, Tennyson's two idylls that are devoted to this subject consistently divulge the characters' states of mind. This allows the reader to understand exactly how Geraint fell into his deplorable state of luxuriousness, as well as how he liberates himself.

Unlike Arthur, who trusts Guinevere until she has completely destroyed his empire, Geraint incorrectly imagines the worst of his wife without a shred of proof. Tennyson blames Geraint's mistrust on his obsession with Enid. Geraint creates a false idol when he worships her "as he loved the light of Heaven" ("The Marriage of Geraint" 5). This adoration causes Geraint to worry obsessively that Enid will become tainted by her friendship with Guinevere, so he removes his wife and himself from the court. At home in Devon, Geraint ignores his responsibilities, preferring to smother his wife with attention:

He compass'd her with sweet observances
And worship, never leaving her, and grew
Forgetful of his promise to the king,
Forgetful of the falcon and the hunt,
Forgetful of the tilt and tournament,

> Forgetful of his glory and his name,
> Forgetful of his princedom and its cares.
> And this forgetfulness was hateful to her.
> ("The Marriage of Geraint" 48-55)

Geraint overhears Enid lamenting his condition while she thinks he is asleep, and he mistakenly believes that she has admitted to having a lover. This imagined affirmation of all his fears makes him decide that he must become a man of brawn to punish his wife. The ridiculous lengths to which Geraint goes, before he believes again that Enid is true reduce him to a brute. As Tennyson shows in his portrayal of Arthur's love of Guinevere that trust should be the basis of marriage, he reveals the opposite in Geraint, who loses his manhood--and even his humanity--when he loses his trust in Enid.

Eventually, after pushing his entirely too tolerant wife nearly to her limit, Geraint is made to understand that she was indeed faithful. He learns to strike the proper balance between his love for Enid and his responsibilities as a man, as the prince of his realm, and, eventually, as a father:

> . . . and in their halls arose
> The cry of children, Enids and Geraints,
> Of times to be; nor did he doubt her more,
> But rested in her fealty, till he crown'd
> A happy life with a fair death, and fell
> Against the heathen of the Northern Sea
> In battle, fighting for the blameless King.
> ("Geraint and Enid" 963-69)

The solution is domestic because "Tennyson never falters from recognizing marriage, home, and child as the central relationships of this life" (Smith 167). Still, Tennyson's intention here is to offset Arthur's lack of attention to Guinevere by showing that the reverse, wife worship, is equally incorrect. Enid is a trustworthy wife and Geraint's immense misunderstanding of her character temporarily destroys his own humanity. When his faith is restored, the benefits are revealed in a happy home with children and a proper knight's death in service to his liege.

ENID

Enid's story in the early legends and in the *Idylls* adheres to the ancient "Patient Griselda" theme. Tennyson does little to change the material, but he does expand it to add Enid's thoughts about her confusion and humiliation. She remains the thoughtful, devoted, innocent wife, willing to suffer her husband's cruelties in silence. Her concerns about the worn and faded dress as improper court attire might be seen as vanity in another woman, but Tennyson makes it evident that Enid is only worried about her husband's possible embarrassment or loss of stature. The selfless Enid is Tennyson's foil to Guinevere, Vivien, Isolt, and Ettarre. Her only fault is a verbal impotence that makes her incapable of suggesting to Geraint that his worship of her not only makes her uncomfortable, but also discredits him. Meaning only that she should accept the uncomfortable duty of explaining to Geraint what people around him are saying, Enid grieves aloud over her husband, who is but half-asleep, "O me, I fear that I am no true wife" ("The Marriage of Geraint" 108).

Tennyson shows here that the ideal wife should be both trustworthy and helpful; when Enid forsakes Geraint as his people lose their respect for him, her silence is mistaken for dishonesty. Geraint mercilessly drives her through the wastelands and allows her to be accosted by Earl Limours and nearly raped by Earl Doorm; all this Enid accepts meekly as chastisement for a crime quite different from the one Geraint thinks she has committed. Still, Tennyson makes it clear that when Enid does not state her concerns for Geraint's welfare, she is culpable for not protecting Geraint. "Geraint and Enid," the fourth idyll, deals with one of the smallest problems caused by Guinevere's infidelity and is also the last idyll that has a happy ending. Enid's friendship with the Queen does not extend to emulating Guinevere's adultery (although Geraint imagines the opposite), so tragedy is averted and a lesson is learned.

PELLEAS

Pelleas, one of the young men knighted to fill the void left by the wandering Grail knights, serves the same capacity in the *Morte* as in the *Idylls*. Tennyson, however, changes the ending of the story to one of tragedy. Pelleas begins in the *Idylls* as an idealistic and handsome young man who longs to join the Order of the Round Table: "Make me thy knight, because I know, Sir King, / All that belongs to knighthood, and I love" ("Pelleas and Ettarre" 8-9). Pelleas hopes to win the golden circlet by jousting in the Tournament of Youth. He wishes to have a lady of his own to whom he can offer this prize and to whom he can adore as he does the Queen:

> And since he loved all maidens, but no maid
> In special, half-awake he whisper'd, "Where?
> O where? I love thee tho' I know thee not.
> For fair thou art and pure as Guinevere,
> And I will make thee with my spear and sword
> As famous--O my Queen, my Guinevere,
> For I will be thine Arthur when we meet."
>   ("Pelleas and Ettarre" 39-45)

This is the ninth idyll, and Tennyson's pattern is set by this point, so we realize as soon as Pelleas indicates his devotion to the Queen that his idealism will be shattered. Although Guinevere is not the woman who breaks Pelleas's heart, the haughty lady Ettarre knows the Queen's secret and, therefore, feels no shame for her own cruel deeds. Pelleas is new to the court and desperately wants to believe in the utopia he imagines Camelot to be. Pelleas's only faults are in not being more selective in his choice of a lover and in devoting himself to the first beautiful woman he sees:

> The beauty of her flesh abash'd the boy,
> As tho' it were the beauty of her soul:
> For as the base man, judging of the good,
> Puts his own baseness in him by default
> Of will and nature, so did Pelleas lend
> All the young beauty of his own soul to hers,
> Believing her.
>   ("Pelleas and Ettarre" 74-80)

This mistake of judging a woman by her physical appearance and assuming that her beauty is also spiritual is the same one Arthur makes with Guinevere. Pelleas is puzzled by Ettarre's unpleasant behavior at first, attributing it to a lady's need to act coyly, but he realizes her true nature fairly quickly. When Pelleas finds Gawain, who has offered to help him to win Ettarre's love, sleeping in Ettarre's arms, he is suddenly enlightened as though this was his rite of passage into the cynical, blighted world of the real Camelot. Pelleas rails against the King who "Hath made us fools and liars" ("Pelleas and Ettarre" 470) until he meets Percivale, who makes it clear that it is the Queen who is false. Thus the completely disheartened youth takes the opposite position just as fiercely as he did with his original adoration of the Queen.

Pelleas, lovesick and angry, rides wildly out of town, only to return in "The Last Tournament" as the evil Red Knight. He maims a churl and sends the man with a message for Arthur:

> Tell thou the King and all his liars, that I
> Have founded my Round Table in the North,
> And whatsoever his own knights have sworn
> My knights have sworn the counter to it--and say
> My tower is full of harlots, like his court,
> But mine are worthier, seeing they profess
> To be none other than themselves--and say
> My knights are all adulterers like his own,
> But mine are truer, seeing they profess
> To be none other; and say his hour is come,
> The heathen are upon him, his long lance
> Broken, and his Excalibur a straw.
>   ("The Last Tournament" 77-88)

This attack on Camelot is heart-rending because it is born of the anguish of a disillusioned youth. Pelleas is not simply complaining about unreasonable moral demands, although this is what Masao Miyoshi suggests: "In the world of 'The Last Tournament' man no longer thinks of himself as being essentially different from the animal. The Red Knight's naturalistic challenge of the hypocrisy of the Round Table is a very modern statement of an age-old dilemma--morality's unreasonable lien on existence" (6-

7). This is an incorrect assessment of the situation because Pelleas was perfectly willing to adhere to the Round Table vows. He originally intended to serve devotedly the King, the Queen, and Ettarre, but once he was taught the true state of affairs at court, he felt that his vows had been secured under false pretenses. The raw, naïve, Pelleas becomes the disgruntled, fierce Red Knight as an outlet for pent-up passion and resentment.

Arthur must respond by crushing the insubordinate youth. The King allows the Red Knight to attempt a swing at him, miss, and fall into the mud before permitting his followers to kill Pelleas:

> . . . then the knights who watch'd him, roar'd
> And shouted and leapt down upon the fall'n;
> There trampled out his face from being known,
> And sank his head in mire, and slimed themselves.
> ("The Last Tournament" 467-70)

Malory does not give Pelleas this dismal ending, but allows him a joyous future as the husband of Nenyve, the powerful Lady of the Lake. Tennyson, faithful to his theme of destruction caused by Guinevere's adultery, obliterates this young knight who was so full of possibility.

ETTARRE

When she first meets Pelleas, the worldly, wealthy Lady Ettarre says to herself, "I have lighted on a fool, / Raw, yet so stale!" ("Pelleas and Ettarre" 108-09). Ettarre allows Pelleas to accompany her to the tournament of youth, because he looks strong and she thinks it likely that he can win glory for her in the jousts. Ettarre wants the golden circlet and the title "Queen of Beauty" so much that she suffers the awkward attentions of Pelleas for a short time. Like Vivien, she toys with a man for her own gain and eventually causes his destruction. After Pelleas wins the tournament and Ettarre reaps the rewards, she is never kind to him again. When Guinevere gently reprimands the lady for her treatment of Pelleas, Ettarre makes it clear that she will suffer no reproach because she knows about the Queen's infidelity:

> Said Guinevere, "We marvel at thee much,
> O damsel, wearing the unsunny face
> To him who won thee glory!" And she said
> "Had ye not held your Lancelot in your bower,
> My Queen, he had not won." Whereat the Queen,
> As one whose foot is bitten by an ant,
> Glanced down upon her, turn'd and went her way.
>   ("Pelleas and Ettarre" 172-78)

Guinevere is unaffected by Ettarre's malicious tongue, and Pelleas reacts similarly to his lady at first, assuming for a while that Ettarre's biting words are some odd form of encouragement. Pelleas is persistent because he is young and knows nothing of women. Ettarre grows to hate Pelleas both for his dogmatism and his purity. Although Tennyson does not explain her reasons, we assume that Ettarre sleeps with Gawain--after he tells her falsely that he has slain Pelleas--to reward him. Malory makes Ettarre's gratitude obvious when she says to Gawayne about Pelleas, "But of all men on lyve I hated hyrn moste, for I could never be quytte of hym. And for ye have slayne hyrn I shall be your woman and to do anythynge that may please you" (169; bk. 4, chap. 23).

Tennyson does not discuss Ettarre's reaction in depth after she discovers that Pelleas is still alive. Instead, as he does at the conclusion of "Gareth and Lynette," Tennyson refers specifically to Malory's treatment of the story:

> And he that tells the tale
> Says that her ever-veering fancy turn'd
> To Pelleas, as the one true knight on earth,
> And only lover; and thro' her love her life
> Wasted and pined, desiring him in vain.
>   ("Pelleas and Ettarre" 482-86)

Tennyson omits the part played here in the *Morte* by Nenyve, who aids Pelleas and punishes Ettarde:

"Loo," seyde the Damesell of the Lake, "ye oughte to be ashamed for to murther suche a knyght," and therewith she threw such an inchauntmente uppon hir that she loved hym so

sore that well-nyghe she was nere oute of hir mynde . . . . So
this lady Ettarde dyed for sorow, and the Damesel of the Lake
rejoysed sir Pelleas, and loved togedyrs duryng their lyfe.

(172; bk. 4, chaps. 23,24)

This pleasant ending for Pelleas is removed in the *Idylls* to
aggravate Pelleas's suffering from Ettarre's treatment. When
Pelleas returns as the Red Knight, the consequences of Ettarre's
actions affect the entire community. Tennyson makes it clear early
in the idyll that Ettarre, aware of Guinevere's conduct, feels no
guilt. Thus once again in the *Idylls*, the blame for a disturbance is
placed on the Queen--even though she was not responsible for the
same problem in the *Morte*, Tennyson uses the Lady Ettarre to
prepare the reader to discover later that Guinevere's rumored
infidelity has indeed occurred. Further, because Ettarre and
Gawain couple adulterously as do Guinevere and Lancelot,
Tennyson shows again the contagious nature of immorality.

GAWAIN

Tennyson's Gawain is not the noble, pure Christian hero of
Sir Gawain and the Green Knight who "watz for gode knawen, and
as golde pured" (Garbáty, *SGGK,* line 633). The Gawain of the
Idylls is similar to the cowardly, discourteous, and lustful Gawain
of the *Morte* except that Tennyson's character is even worse.
Inasmuch as Tennyson omits Malory's chapter in which Launcelot
saves Gwenyvere from being burnt as an adulteress and kills
Gawayne's brothers Gareth and Gaheris in the process, Gawain, in
the *Idylls,* cannot fall back on a redeeming blood loyalty that forces
him to seek vengeance. Tennyson's Gawain is a man of "foolish
words, / a wreckless and irreverent knight" ("The Holy Grail" 852-
53).

When the reader first encounters Gawain in the *Idylls*, he is
not the ideal knight:

With smiling face and frowning heart, a Prince.

. . .

> Sir Modred's brother, and the child of Lot,
> Nor often loyal to his word, and now
> Wroth that the King's command to sally forth
> In quest of whom he knew not, made him leave
> The banquet, and concourse of knights and kings.
>   ("Lancelot and Elaine" 551, 556-60)

Gawain does not want to leave the pleasures of court to ride in the wilderness looking for the unknown winner of the diamond joust (Lancelot), so he only partially fulfills his quest. Although the king orders Gawain to locate and to award the winner personally, this indolent knight, tired of his search, simply leaves the diamond with Elaine. Gawain assumes that the winner, whom he has discovered is Lancelot, will eventually return to Astolat to reclaim his shield. Gawain loiters for some time attempting to overawe and seduce Elaine, the uncosmopolitan maid, with his courtly love talk. When Elaine does not respond, Gawain finally returns to court and is reprimanded by an angry Arthur:

> The seldom frowning King frown'd and replied,
> "Too courteous truly! ye shall go no more
> On quest of mine, seeing that ye forget
> Obedience is the courtesy due to kings."
>   ("Lancelot and Elaine" 710-13)

Irresponsible Gawain is only momentarily silenced by this reproach before rushing off to gossip about the connection he has discovered between Lancelot and Elaine. Gawain continuously proves himself to be yet another untrustworthy member of the honest and true King's household. Tennyson next mentions Gawain when the Grail appears in Arthur's banquet hall: "And Gawain sware, and louder than the rest" ("The Holy Grail" 202) that he would find the holy vessel. These are proud, boastful words since Gawain returns, as before, without accomplishing this second quest. He is not ashamed of not completing his task and swears to pay no heed to anything of a holy nature in the future. Tennyson has so blackened the character of Gawain by this time that the reader is not surprised by the knight's depravity in the next idyll, "Pelleas and

Ettarre." When Gawain offers to help Pelleas win Ettarre's love, he
swears by his uncle the King's highest order:

> . . . here I pledge my troth,
> Yea, by the honour of the Table Round,
> I will be leal to thee and work thy work,
> And tame thy jailing princess to thine hand.
>   ("Pelleas and Ettarre" 333-36)

This oath means nothing to Gawain, who immediately takes
advantage of the situation by having sexual relations with Ettarre.
Tennyson thus indicates that through their shared trait of depravity,
Gawain and Ettarre are characters of equal wickedness. Although
this seems the perfect match, Gawain leaves Ettarre quickly in order
to cause more trouble at the court.[9]

In the *Morte*, Gawayne is wounded twice in the war with
Launcelot but is not killed until the first battle against Mordred.
Tennyson, apparently having no further use for Gawain, allows the
knight to die "in Lancelot's war" and return in spirit to warn the
king by shrieking "to-morrow thou shalt pass away" ("The Passing
of Arthur" 31, 34). Though Malory's Gawayne also warns the king
in a dream, he is believed. In the *Idylls*, Bedivere disparages
Arthur's vision of Gawain because the knight had such a poor
reputation: "Light was Gawain in life, and light in death / Is Gawain,
for the ghost is as the man; / And care not thou for dreams from
him" ("The Passing of Arthur" 56-58). Thus Gawain is forgotten
and never mentioned again in the *Idylls*, Tennyson employs the
character to further his picture of the corruption, deceit, and
immorality in the unsuspecting king's court.

TRISTRAM AND ISOLT

While Malory devotes nearly one-third of his entire text to
the adventures of Trystrame, Tennyson includes this character only
in part of one idyll, "The Last Tournament." Because Tristram is not
nearly as significant in Tennyson's Arthurian poems as he is in those
of Arnold and Swinburne, it seems proper to delay a thorough
examination of Malory's Trystrame until later in this study.

Similarly, Tennyson mentions Isolt only in a passage near the end of the idyll, so a brief discussion of her significance in "The Last Tournament" will simply be included here, rather than in a separate section.

In "The Last Tournament," Tristram is jaded, decadent, and-- although he has recently married Isolt the White of Brittany-- interested only in winning the jousting prize for his lover, Isolt of Britain, wife of King Mark. He mocks everything and seems reborn in Tennyson's work as the king of cynicism at the joust that is dubbed "The Tournament of the Dead Innocence." The spectators remark, "All courtesy is dead" and "the glory of our Round Table is no more" (211, 212) when Tristram wins the ruby necklace. Lancelot, who presides at the ceremony in Arthur's absence, begrudgingly offers the prize: "Not speaking other word than 'Hast thou won? / Art thou the purest, brother?'" (191-92). Tristram, unwilling to accept this tone from a man guilty of the same crime as he, remarks:

> Ay, but wherefore toss me this
> Like a dry bone cast to some hungry hound?
> Let be thy fair Queen's fantasy.
>
> . . .
>
> But O chief knight,
> Right arm of Arthur in the battle-field,
> Great brother, thou nor I have made the world;
> Be happy in thy fair Queen as I in mine.
>   (195-97, 201-04)

Tennyson seems to include Tristram simply to reinforce the loathsomeness of Lancelot's crime. While Lancelot is given some degree of attractiveness as a great soul trapped by uncontrollable desire, Tristram reflects the crass sensuality of a brazen, self-righteous sinner. Little Dagonet, the king's kind and loving fool, is unable to dance when he hears Tristram's song; the refrain of this melody shows the knight's immorality: "Free love--free field--we love but while we may" (275 and 281).

Tennyson reduces the great love story of Tristram and Isolt to a sordid matter of adultery, emblematic of the moral decay of the last days of Camelot. The poet has no sympathy for them and allows the couple no redeeming guilt. Unlike Arnold and Swinburne, Tennyson gives Tristram a death of graphic violence and leaves Isolt existing in terror with her cruel husband. In the *Morte*, Trystrame's death is similar, but it is mentioned only briefly after the fact. The turbulent end of Tennyson's Tristram is expected as reparation for his hedonistic philosophy that glorifies his adulterous relationship with Isolt.

CONCLUSION

Some memorable figures who have been previously omitted because they are of only slight significance to the thesis presented in this volume will be mentioned briefly here. One might wonder why the love of Gareth and Lynette has not been examined in detail. While these characters are interesting, their relationship is standard fare: after a period of turbulence and witty word play, the knight proves his worth to the lady and she gladly accepts his offer of marriage. "Gareth and Lynette" is the second idyll in Tennyson's completed sequence, and because it takes place during the early, ideal days of Camelot, the author uses this charming story to show how a correct love affair should end. Gareth is the perfect knightly hero, and Lynette learns to respect his constancy, service, and bravery.

The story of the twin brothers Balin and Balan in the *Idylls* repeats Tennyson's theme of destruction caused by the Queen's adultery. There have been several fascinating works written that find the brothers to be two sides of the same person destroyed by his inability to integrate his personality. Whether or not this is true, it is clear that Balin worships the Queen and is so disappointed by her impurity that he becomes a savage, dark force who causes the death of his brother and himself.

Dagonet, the King's wise fool, also suffers psychologically from the Queen's crime. This ugly little man is beautiful in his love for and loyalty to Arthur (again the appearance-versus-reality motif). Like the fool in Shakespeare's *King Lear*, Dagonet's big heart is shattered by his very lucid understanding of the horror that surrounds him. When Dagonet clings to Arthur's feet and sobs, "I am thy fool, / And I shall never make thee smile again" ("The Last Tournament" 755-56), the reader feels an overwhelming despair about the state of affairs in Camelot.

The three main Grail Knights, Percivale, Bors, and Galahad, do not have the importance in the *Idylls* that they do in the *Morte*. Tennyson's Percivale must overcome false pride and the temptation of a rich widow in order to see the Grail. Similarly, Bors is allowed just a glimpse of the vessel because he has sinned. The saintly Galahad sits in the Siege Perilous and thus causes the Grail to reappear briefly on earth. He is the only knight pure enough to finish the quest by ascending into the spiritual city. Galahad, cold and withdrawn, is concerned only with his own salvation, so he is not Tennyson's ideal hero. Like King Pelleas, Galahad is a mystic who negates man's dual nature by withdrawing into a purely spiritual realm. His religious zeal results in a death that he welcomes as a rebirth; still, because it causes the entire unfortunate Grail Quest during which so many knights are lost, Galahad's spiritualism is not to be greatly admired.

Another knight of some significance is Bedivere, who is the last living member of the Round Table. This character has not been developed here because he does not have a love relationship (and even seems disloyal at the end to Arthur by twice refusing to throw the sword back into the water), nor does he die. Bedivere is important because he is the link between the past and the future. He tells his story later to strangers who cannot fully comprehend it. Bedivere mourns the King's passing with feelings of great loss, rather like those of Tennyson for his friend Arthur Hallam.

In the *Idylls*, the fall of Camelot is consistently blamed on Guinevere; therefore, Modred does not need to be the arch-villain he is in the *Morte,* and Tennyson has little need to develop his character. We are told several times that the dark, sullen Modred is not Arthur's son, and we are occasionally warned that his intentions are bad. Still, when Modred attempts to usurp the throne, a reader is likely to be surprised, having forgotten that he exists at all.

The one characteristic that connects Tennyson's characters, apart from the fact that all of them are somehow touched by the adultery of Guinevere and Lancelot, is excess. These are people who are unable to comprehend a moderate position. Perhaps this can be explained by J. Philip Eggers's suggestion that the *Idylls* is intended to be a warning against the Victorian tendency to become blindly and overwhelmingly devoted to various causes, like evangelical reform or utilitarian progress (68). Tennyson seems to be intentionally expressing the belief that the total commitment to one purpose, as seen in the characters of the *Idylls*, does not allow for the normal complexities of life:

> Far from catering to a demanding public, Tennyson created such a paradoxical and, in the finest sense, realistic work that any contemporary dogmatist--whether evangelical, atheist, hero-worshipper, aesthete, cynic, or utilitarian-- could see a reflection of his ideals in the story of the Round Table but could not read the *Idylls* as the Bible of his faction without finding that somewhere he had parodied himself. (Eggers 101)

If Tennyson intended to combat the Victorian tendency toward rigidity, he did so by concentrating on the negative effects of obsession. There is no important character in the *Idylls* except Geraint--following his period of turmoil--who is able to achieve a life of proper balance. Tennyson, a poet known for equivocally straddling the middle course between irreconcilable opposites, created in his *Idylls* a series of vignettes that reflect the impossibility of perfect loves or deaths among people who are unable to live both morally and in moderation.

NOTES

1. J. M. Gray's edition of the *Idylls* (New York: Penguin, 1983) notes these biblical allusions.

2. Robert Martin gives a concise explanation of the Hallam connection:

> Although not intended as a literal portrait, the blue-eyed Arthur of Camelot owed a great deal to the blue-eyed Arthur of Cambridge, even to the likeness of the names of places with which they are associated. The *Idylls* were developed out of the "Morte d'Arthur," which was written in grief at Hallam's death; throughout the *Idylls* King Arthur's character seems made to fit that of the dying king in the final idyll, who of course recalls Hallam. (495)

3. Arthur is definitely the child of Uther Pendragon and Ygrene in Malory's *Morte*. In Frederic Madden's edition of Layamon's *Brut* (London: Society of Antiquaries,

1847). However, Arthur's heritage is not so clear because the author is more interested in the same magical or supernatural elements that Tennyson consistently omits:

> Þe time com þe wes icoren:
> Þa wes Arður iboren.
> Sone swa he com an eorðe:
> aluen hine iuengen.
> heo bigolen þat child:
> mid galdere swiðe stronge.
> heoyeuen him mihte:
> to beon bezst alre cnihten.
> heo, yeuen him an oðer þing:
> þat he scolde beon riche king.
> Heo yiuen him þat þridde
> þat he scolde longe libben.
> heo yifen him, þat kine-bern:
> custen swiðe gode.
> þat he wes mete-custi:
> of alle quikemonnen.
> Þis þe alue him yef:
> And al swa þat child iþæh.
>   (Layamon's *Brut,* Madden, 270-78)

("The time came that was chosen, then was Arthur born. So soon as he came on earth, elves took him; they enchanted the child with magic most strong, they gave him might to be the best of all knights; they gave him another thing, that he should be a rich king; they gave him the third, that he should live long; they gave to him, the child, virtues most good, so that he was most generous of all men alive: This the elves gave him and thus the child thrived." [Madden's translation])

4. Gilbert finds this idea of kingship as a natural and internal quality to be a distinctly romantic idea.

5. The feeling that Tennyson saw nature as impelling men downward stems probably from Darwinian theory and is the opposite reaction from George Eliot's humanistic idea of human evolution as a slow glacial movement eventually producing better human beings.

6. Compare, for example, the two final battle scenes to be reminded why so many readers who have discovered Malory find Tennyson's reworkings intolerably bland.

> And uttering this the king
> Made at the man.
> Then Modred smote his liege
> Hard on that helm which many a heathen sword
> Had beaten thin; while Arthur at one blow,
> Striking the last stroke with Excalibur,
> Slew him, and all but slain himself, he fell.
>   (Tennyson, "The Passing of Arthur" 164-69)

And whan sir Mordred saw kynge Arthur he ran untyll hym with hys swerde drawyn in hys honde, and there kyng Arthur smote sir Mordred undir the shylde, with a foyne of hys speare, thorowoute the body more than a fadom. And whan sir Mordred felte that he had hys dethys wounde he threste hymselff with the myght that he had upp to the burre of kyng Arthurs speare, and ryght so he smote hys fadir, kynge Arthure, with hys swerde, holdynge in both hys hondys, uppon the syde of the hede, that the swerde perced the helmet and the tay of the brayne. And therewith Mordred daysshed down starke dede to the erthe. (Malory, Bk. 21, chap. 480, 1237)

7. Between 1861 and 1913, nineteen versions of "The Lady of Shalott" were exhibited at the Royal Academy (Banham and Harris 158). That Tennyson had earlier published (in 1832) another poem dedicated to the same maiden must also be remembered. The lily maid's story, therefore, was already known when "Elaine" was published in 1859. The first poem seems to examine what happens to an artist who abandons a productive seclusion. In "Elaine," however, it is clear that the lady dies of a broken heart (rather than from a curse) because her love for Lancelot is not returned.

8. Catherine Barnes Stevenson's "How It Struck a Contemporary: Tennyson's 'Lancelot and Elaine' and Pre-Raphaelite Art" makes an interesting case that the idyll is "a dramatic embodiment of Tennyson's complex reactions to Pre-Raphaelite art" (8). This article concentrates on the abundance of symbolic, Pre-Raphaelite details Tennyson uses as well as Elaine's attempts to fashion herself in death as the Queen's competitor: "The lily maid insists that she be dressed and laid upon the 'little bed' where she 'died' for love of Lancelot--the virginal analogue not only of the marriage bed she desires but also of the adulterous bed on which the Queen 'dies' with Lancelot" (8-9).

9. This character could not be less like the gracious, courtly hero of *Sir Gawain and the Green Knight*. It is not known if Tennyson read *SGGK*, but Sir Frederic Madden's edition of the text was published in 1847. Although by this year Tennyson had already written "The Passing of Arthur" as "Morte d'Arthur" (1842) with Gawain warning Arthur in a dream, Tennyson could have read *SGGK* before he wrote the other three idylls that include Gawain ("Elaine," 1859, "The Holy Grail," 1869, and "Pelleas and Ettarre," 1869). If so, Tennyson rejected this version in which Gawain is honorable in order to concentrate on increasing the dishonest characteristics found in Malory's Gawayne.

Chapter 3

Matthew Arnold

The Tristram legends seem to have originated in the late-eighth-century Pictish kingdom in Scotland. The original Tristram was probably Drust, son of the Pictish King Talorc, who ruled in Scotland around the year 780 (Barber 74). From here, Tristram legends can be traced through Welsh, Cornish, and Breton sources. In one of her lays, Marie de France mentioned Tristram as an ideal lover, and Chrétien de Troyes also claimed to have written about the hero, although this work is no longer extant. The earliest surviving long poem about Tristan is a version by Thomas of Britain, who wrote at the Plantagenet Court in England after 1150. Thomas was followed by Eilhart von Oberge around 1170, and also by another Norman poet, Béroul, about 1190. Further, from Thomas's *Tristan* a condensed version, *Sir Tristrem*, was composed in Middle English approximately a century later; this is the only other treatment of the subject in Middle English, except for Malory's reworking that comprises about one-third of the *Morte Darthur*. Over many years, the Tristram romances became very complex, "with comic and tragic, savage and civilized, cynical and idealistic parts" (Loomis 82).

When Matthew Arnold published "Tristram and Iseult" in *Empedocles on Etna, and Other Poems* (1852), it was important as the first English retelling of the story in nearly 400 years. Arnold's poem was followed by Richard Wagner's opera *Tristan und Isolde* (first performed in 1865), Tennyson's poem "The Last

Tournament" (1871), and Swinburne's poem *Tristram of Lyonesse* (1882). Arnold wrote a letter to Herbert Hill, dated "5 November 1852," in which he explained that his source for the poem was an article in a French journal:

> I read the story of Tristram and Iseult some years ago at Thun in an article in a French Review on the Romance Literature: I had never met with it before, and it fastened upon me: when I got back to England I looked at the *Morte d'Arthur* and took what I could, but the poem was in the main formed, and I could not well disturb it. If I had read the story first in the *Morte d'Arthur* I should have managed it differently. (Baum 36)

Arnold wrote here that his "poem was in the main formed," but not necessarily that it was even on paper yet. As we shall see, there are many similarities between Arnold's work and Malory's specific version, including several passages that are almost direct quotes; thus the poet must have been somewhat more influenced by the *Morte* than his letter would lead one to believe.

Arnold's primary source has been traced to Théodore de La Villemarqué's "Les poèmes gallois et les romans de la Table-Ronde" from the *Revue de Paris* of 1841 (Carley 2). La Villemarqué's outline, which discusses only a small portion of the extant material about Tristram, was mostly followed by Arnold for his poem's plot, except for a few significant details. In Arnold's poem, Tristram wins the hand of the beautiful Iseult of Ireland for his uncle, King Marc of Cornwall. While Tristram and Iseult are en route to the wedding, they accidentally drink a magic potion created by Iseult's mother for the bride and groom. This powerful drink was intended to ensure an enchanted and eternal love between the married couple. However, since Tristram drinks the potion instead of Marc, he constantly desires Iseult. The Irish princess continues to return Tristram's lust--even after she has married King Marc. When the lovers' liaisons are discovered by Marc, Tristram flees to Brittany, where he marries Iseult of the White Hands, yet constantly pines for Iseult of Ireland. He seeks forgetfulness in knightly adventures and is mortally wounded. His wife tends his wounds, but Tristram sends for Iseult of Ireland and dies in his paramour's arms. Iseult of Ireland falls over the corpse, immediately dying of grief. The lovers are buried together, leaving behind Iseult of the White Hands with her two young children.

Arnold's conclusion is very different from any other treatment of the tale. In La Villemarqué's summary, when Iseult of Ireland is told that Tristram is dead, she runs madly through the streets, finds her dead lover, and dies upon Tristram's corpse. Malory, as almost an afterthought following the Grail Quest, significantly after his conclusion to the Trystrame section, eventually related Trystrame's death at the hands of Mark and La Beale Isode's subsequent death. Neither of these authors mentioned Iseult of Brittany's existence after her husband's death, nor that the couple produced any offspring. Malory made it clear that the marriage of Trystrame and Isode le Blaunche Maynys was never consummated: "And so whan they were a-bed bothe, sir Trystrames remembirde hym of his olde lady, La Beale Isode, and than he toke suche a thoughte suddeynly that he was all dismayed, and other chere made he none [but] with clyppynge and kyssynge. As for [other] fleyshely lustys, sir Trystrames had never ado with hir" (434-35; bk. 8, chap. 36). Tristram and Iseult's children were Arnold's invention.

Particularly because Arnold left Iseult of Brittany in this quiet domestic situation, many critics have found the poem to be typical of the author's period. Commentators who attack the poem as being too Victorian and lacking sufficient medieval atmosphere or attitudes frequently refer to Paull F. Baum's discussion in *Ten Studies* (1958). Baum feels that, because Arnold did not understand the real meaning of the story, the poet wrote a domestic tragedy, rather than the high tragedy that he should have written: "It is obvious that Arnold missed the essential tragic import of the Tristram and Iseult story as we now see it: the tragedy of an overmastering passion . . . in which love transcends all other human relations and in which the lovers are innocent victims of a well-intentioned but accidentally misappropriated magic philtre" (36).

G. Robert Stange in *Matthew Arnold: The Poet as Humanist* (1967) responds to Baum's argument by suggesting that Arnold's more sentimental version is an attempt to give an old work a new interpretation suitable for his audience (271). Arnold, like Tennyson, was not a medieval scholar and seems to have used his poetic imagination to speak to his age. However, because much of the original charm of the Tristram legends is absent from the poem, those among Arnold's contemporary critics who knew the older material did not praise the work (Eggers 131). Even those Victorian readers who knew little of medieval writing--and were thus unlikely to be bothered by modern elements--disliked the work because of its fragmented style of narration (Buckler 124).

In addition to frequent mode shifts, from dramatic dialogue to third-person narrative to first-person reverie, there are also many temporal juxtapositions. Inasmuch as Arnold wrote the first modern version, the love story of Tristram and Iseult was not well known in nineteenth-century England. Readers were likely to become frustrated when they attempted to understand the plot of "Tristram and Iseult" because it is not presented in a linear fashion. Arnold seems to have been purposefully obscure because he may have been unsure of the details himself. Perhaps, however, the constant sequential disruption was intended to make the actual story less important than the codas at the end of each part, in which the narrator discusses small situational concerns in such a way that they become of universal importance.

Part I, "Tristram," is 373 lines of mostly trochaic tetrameter written in a ballad manner. Here the injured and delirious hero recalls the highlights of his love affair with Iseult of Ireland. His wife, who has been tenderly nursing his wound, watches and listens nearby. Part II, "Iseult of Ireland," is 193 lines of dramatic duet in quatrains of alternating trochaic and iambic pentameter, beginning as the lovers are reunited. Their stichomythic conversation ends with their deaths. Part III, "Iseult of Brittany," is 224 lines of quiet, mature heroic couplets that describe the life, one year after the lovers have died, of the widowed Iseult and her children.[1] This innovative style makes the poem often confusing, "but, even so, its poetical accomplishments are real, and it leaves little doubt but that Arnold could have been one of the major poetic craftsmen in the modern tradition" (Buckler 124).

Arnold's poem shows little sympathy for Tristram's predicament. The poet's purpose seems to be reflected in the narrator's coda about "how this fool passion gulls men potently" (III 134). Further, the poem examines the conditions of life that deaden the human soul. The following sections will discuss these themes as they occur in each character's speech and actions, particularly as seen in each figure's responses to love and death.

TRISTRAM

Iseult of Brittany's quiet life in seclusion was mentioned earlier as an ending that is unique to Arnold's version; even more startlingly different is Arnold's point of entry into the narrative. "Tristram and Iscult" opens with its hero weak, feverish, and ranting on his deathbed. All of the important, courageous, and gallant events of Tristram's early career are subordinated, while the poem concentrates on Tristram in middle age, a pathetic, sickly knight. A reader is immediately aware that this is not the same character who was glorified in the medieval romances. Speaking excitedly, while in delirium, Tristram recounts four important episodes of his past life. These flashbacks, intermittently explicated by the narrator, serve to emphasize Tristram's degeneration through passion. The first two of these vividly recalled incidents concern his experiences with Iseult of Ireland, while the last two illustrate his haunting memories of the earlier love affair, after his marriage to Iseult of Brittany.

Arnold subordinated these segments of Tristram's early life to expose the effects of his overwhelming passion. J. Philip Eggers finds that: "the first two segments of Tristram's life seem to imply not only the present and past in his life but the present and past of Europe--its past vital, heroic, and unified; its present disintegrating and deriving its only vital power from the spirit of the past. The poem is the work of a man conscious of living in an age of transition" (133). Arnold's work frequently reflects this unease concerning his era, but nowhere did the poet make this feeling so clear as he did in "The Grande Chartreuse" (1855):

> Wandering between two worlds, one dead,
> The other powerless to be born,
> With nowhere yet to rest my head,
> Like these, on earth I wait forlorn.
>   (85-88)

As Alan H. Roper claims, Arnold sometimes seemed to have had the desire to stand back from reality, watching and waiting for change without facing challenges (289). This may explain why "Tristram and Iseult" begins in such a removed manner, and why the poem retains this feeling of distance even through the seemingly unresolved conclusion.

Arnold concentrated on the knight's "waning time," rather than "his resplendent prime" (I 70, 71), to show that the brief joy of the Irish Iseult's love was not worth the price of a lifetime of banishment from Cornwall. Tristram, weak and pale, is unable to use his green hunter's dress and his golden harp, the two items that generally characterize this knight when he appears in medieval romances; these items lie untouched on Tristram's bed, relinquished with his youth. His wife stands by the dying fire, watching and pitying Tristram, as the knight suffers the effects of a tyrannous and obsessive passion. Tristram does not realize that the Iseult he married is even in the room, and he compulsively recounts aspects of his earlier life: Iseult of Ireland asking Tristram to pledge her for courtesy with the drugged wine; the lovers discovered during a winter garden walk, and Tristram fleeing after one last kiss; the brave knight seeking to overcome his passion through challenges and, thereby, being wounded in King Arthur's war against Rome; and Tristram seeking refuge and solace in a forest, only to see Iseult of Ireland's face when the moonlight shines upon the water of a spring. The narrator's enlargement upon Tristram's ranting is the bulk of Arnold's exposition in "Tristram and Iseult." Obviously, Arnold's omissions were intended to simplify the material and to focus attention upon Tristram in his last days, but a reader unfamiliar with the story would be likely to misunderstand exactly what is occurring.

Following his fevered recollections, Tristram notices that his wife is in the chamber, and he speaks a few words to her that are much kinder than the heartless ones he spoke to her at the poem's beginning: "Ah! not the Iseult I desire" (I 8). Odd though it seems, Tristram speaks harshly to his lover Iseult when she arrives, weary from her sea voyage:

> Thou art come at last, then, haughty Queen!
> Long I've waited, long I've fought my fever;

> Late thou comest, cruel thou hast been.
>   (II 2-4)

This chilly welcome is no celebration, but proves even more the suffering and agitation caused by an adulterous union. The passion of Tristram and Iseult has long since passed, and there is in the poem no outpouring of ecstasy caused by romantic love. Tristram finally accepts his Queen's arrival, but with a weary questioning of her faithfulness to him.

Iseult of Ireland quickly explains her loyalty to Tristram, but once he is satisfied and relaxed, his death immediately follows. Thus, less than halfway through the poem, the hero departs to his eternal rest, and the remainder of the verses are devoted to the other characters' lives without him. Before Tristram dies, he explains that his doleful life and quick passing were to be expected:

> This is what my mother said should be,
> When the fierce pains took her in the forest,
> The deep draughts of death, in bearing me.
> "Son," she said, "thy name shall be of sorrow;
> Tristram art thou call'd for my death's sake."
>   (II 82-86)

This section distinctly echoes the *Morte*'s version in which Trystrame's mother, Elyzabeth, says as she is dying after giving birth:

> A, my lytyll son, thou haste murtherd thy modir! And therefore I suppose thou that arte a murtherer so yonge, thow arte full lykly to be a manly man in thyne ayge; and bycause I shall dye of the byrth of the, I charge my jantyllwoman that she pray my lorde, the kynge Melyodas, that whan he is crystened let calle hym Trystrams,[2] that is as much to say as a sorowfull byrth. (372; bk. 8; chap. 1)

Although Arnold includes a passage very much like the one in the *Morte*, he did not seem to share Malory's belief that the sorrowful life of Trystram was fated or predestined. The poet also did not particularly stress, as earlier writers did, the idea of Tristram and Iseult's passion being simply the result of their ingestion of the enchanted drink. Indeed, Arnold's narrator yet again, in his maddening way, comments on anything else rather than discuss the exact causes of Tristram's problems. It can easily seem that "Tristram and Iseult" has as many ambiguities as the whole of Tennyson's *Idylls*. To discover what message Arnold may have intended to portray through the character of Tristram--beyond the idea that passion is deadly--one must examine the other characters.

ISEULT OF IRELAND

Arnold devotes the second part of "Tristram and Iseult" to Iseult of Ireland, "the most passionate heroine he ever conceived" (Stange 220). Just as Arnold invented Tristram's brown hair, he assigned raven locks and dark eyes to the Irish princess; this makes her a more perfect foil for Arnold's golden-haired Iseult of Brittany, and therefore, "in the opposition of the two Iseults there is a hint of the classic Victorian concern about the Eve/Mary contrast" (Carley 3). The first Iseult is haughty, beautiful, and full of movement, while the second Iseult is sweet, pale, and static.

Arnold did not overtly judge Iseult of Ireland,[3] but simply showed the effects of the violent sexual passion that "consumed her beauty like a flame, / And dimmed it like the desert-blast" (II 134-35). Marc's Queen arrives at Tristram's bedside full of anguish as well as excuses for her late arrival. She announces that she has been detained in "royal state with Marc, my deep-wronged husband" (II 45). Tristram questions her fidelity since she has been with "silken courtiers whispering honeyed nothings" (II 47). Iseult claims that she has been true to Tristram and equally miserable:

> Ah, on which, if both our lots were balanced,
> Was indeed the heaviest burden thrown--
> Thee, a pining exile in thy forest,
> Me, a smiling queen upon my throne?
>
> Vain and strange debate, where both have suffered,
> Both have pass'd a youth consumed and sad,

> Both have brought their anxious day to evening,
> And have now short space for being glad!
> (II 49-56)

Both lovers have been wretched while apart, and the reader remains uncertain about how much of their passion stems from natural feelings of love and how much is the effect of the magic potion. La Villemarqué blames their lust entirely on enchantment, and Malory, in his much longer explanation, does the same. Malory, however, constantly refers to the relationship in glorified terms as a connection bringing enormous bliss to the lovers: "And to telle the joyes that were betwyxte La Beall Isode and sir Trystramys, there ys no maker can make hit, nothir no harte can thynke hit, nother no penne can wryte hit, nother no mowth can speke hit" (493; bk. 9, chap. 17). Clearly, Arnold's position is the opposite of Malory's.

The lovers do indeed "have now short space for being glad" (II 56); immediately after Iseult has comforted Tristram, he realizes that he is dying. Iseult, despite the immorality of their entire relationship or her pagan association with sorcery, demands that Tristram ask heaven for help: "Call on God and on the holy angels!" (II 79). In the next line, Iseult, more characteristically for one so lacking in Christian spirituality, utters an oath: "Christ! he is so pale" (II 80). Tristram pleads with Iseult, asking that she not go far from his grave; with this for encouragement, Iseult kisses Tristram and dies with him.

The long-separated, middle-aged lovers have been wasted by passion, but are granted a final tranquil moment in death. The proud, petulant, and imperious Irish Iseult is relieved of the stale court life in which she has been unable to hide her secret:

> And the dames whispered scoffingly:
> "Her moods, good lack, they pass like showers!
> But yesternight and she would be
> As pale and still as wither'd flowers,
> And now to-night she laughs and speaks
> And has a colour in her cheeks;
> Christ keep us from such fantasy!"
> (II 124-130)

A great change comes over Cornwall's Queen when she is relieved of the tormented passion that has consumed her life and looks. The narrator describes how this release returns her former beauty:

> And though the bedclothes hide her face,
> Yet were it lifted to the light,
> The sweet expression of her brow
> Would charm the gazer, till his thought
> Erased the ravages of time,
> Filled up the hollow cheek, and brought
> A freshness back as of her prime
> So healing is her quiet now.
> (II 136-43)

Iseult of Ireland becomes, with death, more like her former rival, Iseult of Brittany.

It has been noted that the narrator's first line, "What knight is this so weak and pale" (I 9), unmistakably echoes Keats's "La Belle Dame sans Merci" (Carley 2). This connection is ended when Iseult of Ireland is destroyed along with her exhausted knight. Part II is the most dramatic part of "Tristram and Iseult" and, according to A. Dwight Culler, is not as good as the others:

> It is the least successful part of the poem, and I think one may say that it is intended to be . . . . It presents the fact of a violent sexual passion, and the meaning of the poem consists in the attitude taken up by the poem as a whole toward this fact. As Empedocles spoke and then leaped into the volcano, so the lovers do the only thing left to them to do--die and leave the field to Iseult of Brittany. (145)

Their bodies are taken by ship to Cornwall, where they are buried in state by King Marc, who now regrets his having separated the lovers. The final part of the poem barely mentions the lovers, but focuses upon the lonely life of Iseult of Brittany.

ISEULT OF BRITTANY

Arnold treated Iseult of Brittany with unprecedented expansiveness by devoting all of part III of "Tristram and Iseult" to her life without her husband. The reader only once before saw her interact with Tristram, when he awakened from delirium to find that she had been in the chamber, listening to his excited talk about Iseult of Ireland. To her credit, Iseult of Brittany reacts as the perfect Patient Griselda by sympathetically regarding her husband:

> Not with a look of wounded pride,
> A look as if the heart complained
> Her look was like a sad embrace;
> The gaze of one who can divine
> A grief, and sympathize.
> (I 320-24)

Iseult of the White Hands is much kinder to her husband in "Tristram and Iseult" than she is in most earlier sources, where we find the incident of the white and black sails[4]: Tristram, dying of a wound from a poisoned lance, sends a messenger to notify Iseult of Ireland that her lover requires that she come to him. So that Tristram can assess the result of his plea from a distance, the messenger is instructed to display a white sail on his return voyage if the Irish Iseult is accompanying him, black if she is not. Iseult of Brittany, finally furious about her husband's long-term affair, overhears the plan; when Tristram asks his wife what color the sails are, she lies by reporting that the sails are black. Tristram dies immediately of a broken heart, and Iseult of Ireland, arriving soon after, expires on his corpse.

This "pitiful malice" (Dunlop 206) felt and acted upon by Iseult of Brittany is not in the *Morte*; however, it is mentioned, without being fully developed, by La Villemarqué. By ignoring this portion of the Tristram legend, Arnold created an Iseult of Brittany devoid of treacherous intentions and one able to arouse the reader to sympathetic feeling. We pity the wife who loved and nursed her husband, bore his children, and yet had to endure his constant obsession with another woman. Iseult of Brittany is presented in the poem before her rival Iseult, and this wife is described by the narrator in words that would particularly appeal to a Victorian audience:

> Who is this snowdrop by the sea?--
> I know her by her mildness rare,
> Her snow-white hands, her golden hair;
> I know her by her rich silk dress,
> And her fragile loveliness
> The sweetest Christian soul alive,
> Iseult of Brittany.
>
> (I 49-55)

Tristram's parting words concerning Iseult of Brittany also reinforce this idea of her as an understanding Christian wife: he tells his lover Iseult to find his wife and "speak her fair, she is of royal blood! / Say, I willed so, that thou stay beside me-- / She will grant it; she is kind and good" (I 94-96). This passage echoes Malory's explanation of why Trystrame married the second Isode despite the enchantment that kept him eternally tied to the Irish Isode:

> So by the grete meanes of the kynge and his sonne there grewe grete love betwyxte Isode and sir Trystrames, for that lady was bothe goode and fayre, and a woman of noble bloode and fame. And for because that sir Trystrames had suche chere and ryches and all other plesaunce that he had allmoste forsakyn La Beale Isode. (434; bk. 8, chap. 36)

In the *Morte*, Isode le Blaunche Maynys is encouraged to marry sir Trystrame by her father, King Howell of Bretayne, and by her brother. La Villemarqué mentions Iseult's father, but omits her brother, while Arnold calls her "the lovely orphan child" (I 92). The poet's change of this character's family situation seems intended to increase the pathos of her lonely existence. A reader's pity for the wife would also be heightened by the presence of her two children, who are not noted in any other source of the Tristram story.

Arnold's description of the Irish Iseult as proud and petulant is unlikely to encourage an audience's affection. Further, the focus upon the long-suffering wife, whose children are not of much importance to their father, ensures a reader's distaste for Tristram. Clearly Arnold, like Tennyson, did not intend for adulterous love to be viewed as attractive. In the third part, Iseult of Brittany becomes the central figure of the poem, and it is this character who is likely to remain in a reader's memory and to be recalled as the most likable. Through the addition of details about her domestic life and activities with her children, Arnold made Iseult of Brittany much more substantial than her rival queen. In Arnold's poem, "the two Iseults represent the contrast between passion and devoted serviceable love; between a strained world of violent action and tranquil retreat" (Stange 257). Neither woman is perfect, but Iseult of Brittany is treated more sympathetically.

One year after the lovers' deaths, left with only her children and servants in the seaside castle, Iseult seems lonely and languid. The narrator asks the obvious questions without answering them:

> And is she happy? Does she see unmoved
> The days in which she might have lived and loved
> Slip without bringing bliss slowly away,
> One after one, to-morrow like to-day?
> Joy has not found her yet, nor ever will--
> Is it this thought which makes her mien so still,
> Her features so fatigued, her eyes, though sweet,
> So sunk, so rarely lifted save to meet
> Her children's?
>   (III 64-72)

Iseult's only joy is playing on the heath with her children. The poem ends with the three walking among the hollies on a winter's day as Iseult tells her children "an old-world Breton history" (III 37), the tale of Merlin and Vivian.[5]

This interpolated tale is puzzling because it seems out of place, distracting, and a very strange conclusion to the poem. Paull F. Baum believes that Arnold included the story as a diversion because the poet wished to end with a flourish; this critic also feels that "such a story, adorned with much descriptive detail but divested of its sinister elements, might very well amuse little children" (51). William E. Buckler finds that if the story does relieve sadness, it is through terror (125). The story of Merlin's horrible fate does not seem a particularly appropriate topic to relate to small children, but entertaining youngsters was not Arnold's intention; the storytelling session is more a type of therapy for Iseult of Brittany.

If we view such stories as assuming "the function of medieval *exempla*" (Stange 276), we are left with the feeling that passion creates a state of death-in-life. Applied to Arnold's characters, Merlin is Tristram and the fair Vivian seems, at first, to correspond with the enchanting Iseult of Ireland. However, because Arnold included few of Vivian's physical characteristics, the specific mention of her "white right hand" (III 174) intentionally connects the character with Iseult of Brittany. This connection is strengthened when we remember that the wife Iseult did, in effect, imprison Tristram through marriage and thus hasten his death by parting him from his lover, his raison d'être.

Iseult's judgments on her marriage are "emotions recollected in bitter tranquility" (Buckler 121), and her sorrow may well be transmuted into the aesthetic experience of storytelling. Arnold used Malory's darker view of Merlin's story and omitted La Villemarqué's more softened version, in which Vivian is eternally remorseful for the damage that she does to Merlin.[6] Malory explained Nenyve's enchantment of Merlin by having his narrator report that "she was ever passinge wery of hym" (126; bk. 4, chap. 1). Arnold again distinctly echoed Malory in the last line of "Tristram and Iseult" with Iseult's explanation of Vivian's treachery: "For she was passing weary of his love" (III 224). After having a year to recall Tristram's limitations as a spouse, Arnold's Iseult may believe that she is well rid of a husband who was not of much use to her or her children. Iseult's passive life with Tristram gradually eroded any spirit she might have had before their marriage--leaving her trapped in a state like that of Merlin. Perhaps Iseult's telling of this particular tale indicates her understanding of her own confined state and suggests her possible future renewal, as well as the idea that she is now content to have lost Tristram.

Arnold leaves Iseult of Brittany's feelings ambiguous. All that is certain is that her feelings of weary melancholy, bordering on ennui, are the result of Tristram's passion for another woman and his death. Grief would be acceptable, but Iseult's lack of vibrance, attitude of emptiness, and telling of the story of Merlin and Vivien are disconcerting.

CONCLUSION

If it is true that "Arnold's poetry almost invariably implies the solution to the problems which it poses" (Roper 289), then the solutions in "Tristram and Iseult" are to be found in the narrator's commentary. The narrator is forceful and involved, but always obscure and ambivalent, even when he seems most vehement (Miyoshi 9). His formal, archaic, minstrel-like tone frames many of the conversational speeches with undramatic, explicit exposition. This character presents the poem's conflict in his opening segment:

> There were two Iseults who did sway
> Each her hour of Tristram's day;
> But one possess'd his waning time,
> The other his resplendent prime.
> (I 68-71)

What makes Arnold's narrator of such interest and has created so much controversy among critics, are the codas at the end of each of the poem's three main sections. These codas widen the poem's range by making a moral application somewhat clearer and more universal. Arnold used the narrator's position in numerous other ways as well:

> It kept the poet wholly effaced; it cast in the narrator role, implanted in the text, a qualified commentator who could be expected to see vividly, tell crisply, ruminate relevantly, speculate on the significance of the total action with appropriate circumspection and depth, interpret worthily but not infallibly; and it brought the poet and the reader into analogous roles-watching a fascinating watcher watch. (Buckler 123)

Arnold's commentator speaks with a detachment that borders on dramatic irony when, at the end of each part, he "emphasizes the contrast between transient suffering and permanent art" (Stange 266).

In the first coda, the narrator moves from watching the children sleep to the visions their imaginations could create if they viewed the night landscape from a window. Ultimately, however, the commentator notes that these dazzling observations are unnecessary because the children are able to see more exciting prospects in their dreams. In the second coda, the narrator looks at a tapestry wherein the timeless figure of a huntsman apparently comes to life and looks down at the dead lovers (reminding one of the narrator in "The Grande Chartreuse" and showing that this same problem of immobility can exist in another period). The hunter, on a chase with his dogs, pauses to wonder at the sight of what he thinks is a sleeping knight with his lady next to him, kneeling in prayer by the bed. The huntsman does not realize that death has overtaken the couple, and the narrator says to the figure trapped in the tapestry:

> O Hunter! and without a fear
> Thy golden-tassel'd bugle blow,
> And through the glades thy pastime take--
> For thou will rouse no sleepers here!
> For these thou seest are unmoved;
> Cold, cold as those who lived and loved
> A thousand years ago.
>   (II 187-93)

This fusion of artistic forms creates an aesthetic effect of harmony between immediacy and distance. The last two lines give the poem's present a millennial rhythm that fuses especially well with the huntsman's interesting angle of vision.

The narrator's third coda seems to contain the heart or essential meaning of "Tristram and Iseult." Although further action is denied the characters of Arnold's ancient story, those of the modern world must still face a similar situation. It is not suffering that stunts our ability to see, feel, and grow:

> No, 'tis the gradual furnace of the world,
> In whose hot air our spirits are upcurl'd
> Until they crumble, or else grow like steel--
> Which kills in us the bloom, the youth, the spring--
> Which leaves the fierce necessity to feel,
> But takes away the power--this can avail,
> By drying up our joy in everything,
> To make our former pleasures all seem stale.
> (III 119-126)

This seems to represent Arnold's version of Carlyle's "Centre of Indifference": "He [Arnold] is one of the first in English to take into himself the assertion of the 'Everlasting No,' that modern inference from the breakdown of classical metaphysics, to the effect that life lacks moral purpose and that the universe is not merely mechanical or neutral, but finally, hostile" (DeLaura 41). The solution that seems suggested is an embracement of storytelling and other expressions of imagination. In this way, "the poem is a reaction against the 'unpoetrylessness' of Arnold's age and is a positive statement--even if it begins and ends with melancholy poignancy" (Carley 6).

Further, it is in this third part that Arnold's narrator partially unveils his views about the adulterous relationship between Tristram and Iseult--or, at least, his feelings about those who respond only to "some tyrannous single thought":

> Call it ambition, or remorse, or love
> This too can change us wholly, and make seem
> All which we did before, shadow and dream.
> And yet, I swear, it angers me to see
> How this fool passion gulls men potently;
> Being in truth, but a diseased unrest,
> And an unnatural overheat at best.
> (III 130-36)

The narrator's commentary suggests that both the "gradual furnace" of the world and the "single thought" are equally undesirable and destructive. Iseult of Brittany is an example of the former, Iseult of Ireland of the latter. Tristram has been destroyed by the worst possible combination of the two.

Arnold used the power of artifice in an ancient tale to yield new meanings by enhancing our understanding of contemporary life. The slow destructive power of the world is just as debilitating as the consumptive force of passion. The poem's balanced opposition, shown in the contrast between two kinds of women and two kinds of love, is disturbing. Arnold revealed that this dichotomy can be neutralized through imaginative power combined with the serenity that this power can create. The poet's message seems to have been that moderation and an understanding of the larger issues treated in the universal themes of art are the essential aspects of a fulfilling life. Love should not be a debilitating obsession or a force that gradually burns away all spirit, leaving only melancholy.

NOTES

1. A. Dwight Culler in *Imaginative Reason: The Poetry of Matthew Arnold* (1966) argues that these varied poetic forms are intended to comment upon the contents of each part. Further, he finds the first part to be written like Coleridge's *Christabel*, the second like many of Byron's lyrics, and the third like the more polished works by Keats or by Cowper (144-45).

2. The name *Tristram* is derived from the Latin word *tristitia* meaning "sorrow" (Buckley and Woods 43n).

3. Arnold does not include Iseult's treachery to her maid Brangion, who, in earlier legends, was forced to take Iseult's place in King Mark's bed and was then given by Iseult to two murderers to ensure her silence. This incident is omitted by Malory and La Villemarqué, so Arnold may not have known about it.

4. The episode of the sails as a signal of success or failure seems to have been derived from the Theseus legend of classical Greek mythology. Also involved in early Tristram legends is a half-bestial adversary who demands tribute every seven years and is very similar to the Minotaur slain by Theseus (Barber 74).

5. Critics have not previously noted that the description of the tale of Merlin and Vivien as an "old-world Breton history" is anachronistic. Merlin is always associated with the court of King Arthur, as are Tristram and his two Iseults. (Tristram is known as a fine competitor in Arthur's jousts and as a close friend of Lancelot.) Therefore, it is odd that Iseult tells a story "she gleaned from

Breton grandames, when a child" (III 108), because Merlin and Vivian are her contemporaries. Arnold may have been confused about this point, since he was not an Arthurian scholar. Perhaps, however, Arnold was simply too concerned about the importance of recalling ancient stories in general, and reviewing the implications of the Merlin and Vivian story in particular, to resist including this specific tale as one passed down through several generations.

6. It is possible that Arnold read La Villemarqué's article about Merlin and Vivian called "Viste au tombeau de Merlin" at the same time that he discovered the one concerning Tristram and Iseult that so influenced him.

Chapter 4

William Morris

In 1858, when William Morris published his first volume of poetry, *The Defence of Guenevere and Other Poems*, he had not yet fully developed his auxiliary talents as "artist, pattern designer, weaver, dyer, expert on medieval manuscripts, illuminator, printer, businessman, political agitator, book collector, and translator" (Hodgson, *Romances* 13). He was a young man of only twenty-four who brought his poetical characters thoroughly to life through his imagination, his familiarity with the ideas of Dante Gabriel Rossetti and other Pre-Raphaelites, his wide reading of poetry, and his acute understanding of medievalism. The volume's initial four poems are Arthurian, derived from Malory's *Morte*: "The Defence of Guenevere," "King Arthur's Tomb," "Sir Galahad, A Christmas Mystery," and "The Chapel in Lyoness." Four other works included in the volume mention Arthurian characters: "Golden Wings," "Near Avalon," "Sir Peter Harpdon's End," and "A Good Knight in Prison." All but the last poem briefly refer to various figures from Camelot as dead, but well remembered. In "A Good Knight in Prison," the protagonist, Sir Guy, is a contemporary of Launcelot and is rescued by him.

Also around the time that the poems were written for this 1858 volume, Morris began a poem called "The Maying of Guenevere"; the work survives as a fragment, although Morris never published it. This poem concerns the frustration of Mellyagraunce, who loves Guenevere even though she ridicules him for his attentions. Apparently Morris intended to write an epic Arthuriad, beginning with "The Maying of Guenevere" and ending with "King Arthur's Tomb," but the plan never came to fruition.

Morris's volume appeared a year before the first series of Tennyson's *Idylls of the King* (1859). He knew the early Tennyson poems: "Morte d'Arthur," "Sir Galahad" (which he disliked), and the fragment "Sir Launcelot and Queen Guinevere." Only the last--with its images of spring and description of the passionate kiss of the lovers, seems to have influenced him, and the appearance of the *Idylls* may well have made him abandon his own plan for an Arthurian cycle. (Silver, *Romance* 196)

Two other extant Arthurian fragments written by Morris are "Sir Palomydes' Quest" (about this knight's search for the Questing Beast and his love for the Irish Iseult) and "Saint Agnes [sic] Convent" (about Iseult of Brittany's unhappy life without Tristram and her pleasant memories of him).

The Defence of Guenevere and Other Poems also contains works about non-Arthurian medieval subjects; these poems stem from Morris's reading of Lord Berners's translation of Jean Froissart's *Chronicle* (1369-c. 1400). Other works in the volume are mostly about various subjects and characters from fantasy, such as Rapunzel. Taken as a whole, the volume is depressingly emphatic on disillusionment, imprisonment, and death. There is a sparkling and colorful facade of exciting places, times, and characters, but this facade can only fleetingly mask darker meanings. Victorian critics, for the most part, responded unfavorably; these early readers complained "of the poems' obscurity, formlessness and general lack of relevance to contemporary life" (Hodgson, *Romance* 50). Morris was so taken aback by this harsh criticism that he published nothing more for the next nine years.

Today several works from *The Defence of Guenevere and Other Poems* are typically included in most anthologies of Victorian poetry; modern critics frequently write commentary that would be in agreement with Philip Henderson's feeling that this was Morris's "most passionately felt book," of "a flaming imaginative intensity he was never again to recapture" (Morris 29). The book was dedicated "To My Friend, Dante Gabriel Rossetti, Painter," and Rossetti's influence can be felt in the vividness, the symbolism, and the bright, clear word pictures. It is evident that Morris was also influenced by the Romanticism of Keats and the lyricism of Tennyson. However, the most obvious stylistic influence stems from Browning, inasmuch as so many of this volume's poems employ the dramatic-monologue technique. Morris's particular contribution to this hybrid of styles "was in the directness, bluntness, and violence--the brutality with which he rendered his pictures of the Middle Ages" (Lang 508).

Morris's poems of this first volume have been called "the last true and uncorrupted works of the Romantic revolt," a revolt brought about because the Romantic poets were forced into a dream world of imagination by the advances of industrial capitalism and the triumph of a philistine middle class (Thompson 78). Charlotte H. Oberg in *A Pagan Prophet: William Morris* (1978) agrees that Morris was a Romantic in this early stage of his career:

> It is actually rather ironic that the cliché about Morris that is given widest circulation is that he was at once an interpreter and champion of the Middle Ages, for, though he was indisputably an authority on many aspects of that period, his turn of mind was never medieval, but something at once older and more modern: he was a pagan and a Rousseauvian romantic, a lover of the earth and mankind, whose innate goodness was the infallible sign of his birthright--of his kinship, of his identity, with the natural world. (158-59)

In the discussion to follow, we will see few aspects of Morris's paganism, for it is only his completely Arthurian poems that concern us here, and these works reflect a remarkable degree of Christian spirituality. Oberg's comment about the poet's identification with the natural world, however, will be underscored by this study. As the people of the Middle Ages were, of necessity, so greatly concerned with the more rigorous or environmental aspects of life, Morris's poems show a fidelity to the medieval period (for example, in their frequent mentions of weather conditions), while they simultaneously reflect important aspects of Romanticism.

Morris's four Arthurian poems, although they often deviate in details from their source, are true to the spirit of Malory's *Morte*. As an undergraduate at Oxford, Morris bought Robert Southey's 1817 edition of the *Morte*, and it quickly became the most important book in the world to him (L. Stevenson 132). The poems are all original because Morris exposed and examined the motivations Malory mentioned, but did not amplify. Like most writers, Morris uses his source as a springboard from which to elaborate his own ideas and concerns, which, in this case, develop around the fine line between human love in its highest form and this same love as it dissolves into sin. Because it involves adultery and the disintegration of an entire kingdom, Morris showed the love of Launcelot and Guenevere, explored in the first two poems, as clearly wrong; still, Morris examined two ideas prevalent in medieval society that would mitigate a guilty verdict against these famous lovers: human love should be enjoyed on earth as a gift from God, and maintaining the code of courtly love is honorable. Particularly in "King Arthur's Tomb," Morris stressed the difficulty of recognizing correct and incorrect types of love; the poet did this by showing the characters near the end of their human lives and focusing on Guenevere's concern about the afterlife. The two Galahad poems reflect the reverse problem: this knight, as God's chosen one, is assured of immortality, but Galahad wonders if the heavenly rewards for his chaste, loveless life will be worth the loneliness and anguish he has experienced on earth.

Morris's Arthurian poems are complex and, in parts, ambiguous. In this aspect, as well as in spirit, Morris was faithful to Malory's rendering of the tragedy because the medieval writer was frequently unclear about the meanings of his many interwoven tales. Morris recaptures the *Morte*'s richness by including many of its details, although he dramatizes only minute sections of Malory's text. Morris explores a variety of reactions from characters who are involved in the downfall of Camelot, but it is clear, as it is in the *Morte*, that its ultimate destruction is the product of many different forces. Like Malory (and completely unlike Tennyson), Morris did not assign blame. The poems diverge from the *Morte* in that they go beyond a simple report of events to an examination of the possible psychological motivations behind the actions of important characters.

Many of Morris's revelations about these psychological motivations include views of characters' sexual frustrations, and it is this aspect of the poems that may partially explain their unpopularity among Victorian readers, who had already been introduced to some of Tennyson's more diluted and sanitized Arthurian works. Further, Morris's darker vision could not be easily accepted in his period:

> An era, such as the Victorian, lacking a major war or myth of defeat (such as the Confederate States of America), committed to the ideology of progress, and reticent to the point of inanity on sex, could not accommodate the vision of a poet obsessed with strife, defeat and sex. It is an attitude impossible to project in contemporary nineteenth-century terms. (Berry 280)

Perhaps it is the sexuality of the works that makes them more enjoyable to modern readers, but Carol Silver notes other attractions:

> Unlike the early prose tales and much of Morris's other verse, the works of his 1858 volume, *The Defence of Guenevere and Other Poems,* are replete with qualities which appeal to twentieth-century readers. Brief, intense, concentrated distillations of experience, these poems often contain the conversational tone, the idiosyncratic idiom, and the dramatic effects that excite modern readers. (Silver, *Romance*, 13)

Morris's Arthurian poems are also filled with an attractive irony because the writer juxtaposed the creative and destructive forces of love until these forces became a labyrinth of intertwined emotions. The poet did this largely through an examination of human sexuality that is mostly symbolic and lacks the overt eroticism we will note in Swinburne's Arthurian works. Morris counterpoised the freshness of romantic love with its aftermath of harsh, stark guilt in a manner that is poignant in its sincerity. Morris's characters experience heightened feelings of passion--far surpassing the poems of Tennyson and Arnold in this regard--that make decisions for sexual abstinence more difficult.

Meredith B. Raymond, in "The Arthurian Group in *The Defence of Guenevere and Other Poems*" (1966), notes that Morris's four Arthurian poems form two pairs of diptychs with "The Defence of Guenevere" and "King Arthur's Tomb" as the first and "Sir Galahad, a Christmas Mystery" and "The Chapel in Lyoness" as the second. These poems can be appreciated separately, but understanding is heightened when they are viewed as pairs. Each work will be examined individually here, but it should be understood that coupling strengthens this particular reading. Also, when read together, these four poems form a coherent whole.

"THE DEFENCE OF GUENEVERE"

"The Defence of Guenevere" begins *in medias res* with "But," a word that defines the ambiguity of Guenevere's entire situation, as well as her defense. The poem maintains a degree of uncertainty throughout about Guenevere's degree of guilt and in which particular situations she actually committed adultery. Her justifications are constantly tainted by admissions of some culpability. Guenevere's point is that both she and Launcelot were sinless on the night in question, but this innocence is undercut each time she returns to her refrain, lines containing a reminder that there were probably many other occasions when the Queen and her knight were not blameless:

> Nevertheless you, O Sir Gauwaine, lie,
> Whatever may have happened through these years,
> God knows I speak truth, saying that you lie.
> (46-48)

If Morris is following Malory's version of the story--which, except for a few details, he seems to do--then this ambiguity stems from his source. The occasion from the *Morte* that is examined in the poem is the second time that the Queen is accused of adultery, and the second time that she is very close to being burned at the stake. In the *Morte* we are told that Gwenyvere is shriven by a priest, but we are not privy to her confession or repentance. The Queen does not speak at all and is rescued by her knight just as the kindling about her body is about to be ignited.

Although Morris appointed Gauwaine as Guenevere's accuser,[1] this knight is the Queen's strong supporter on the same occasion in the *Morte*. Despite the fact that his brother, Aggravayne, and his sons, Florens and Lovell, were killed trying to trap Launcelot, Malory's Gawayne movingly tries to persuade the King to spare his Queen:

> "My lorde Arthure, I wolde counceyle you nat to be over hasty, but that ye wolde put hit in respite, thys jougemente of my lady the quene, for many causis. One ys thys, thoughe hyt were so that sir Launcelot were founde in the quenys chambir, yet hit myght be so that he cam thydir for none evyll. For ye know, my lorde," seyde sir Gawayne, "that my lady the quene hath oftyntymes ben gretely beholdyn unto sir Launcelot, more than to ony othir knyght; for oftyntymes, he hath saved her lyff and done batayle for her whan all the courte refused the quene. And peraventure she sente for hym for goodnes and for none evyll, to rewarde hyrn for his good dedys that he had done to her in tymes past . . . . My lady, your quene, ys to you both good and trew."[2] (1175; bk. 20, chap. 7)

Perhaps Morris did not simply confuse the names of Aggravayne and Gauwaine as has been suggested (Perrine 235). In the *Morte* Launcelot accidentally kills two more of Gawayne's brothers, Garherys and Gareth, in the madness that accompanies his rescue of the Queen. Gareth was Gawayne's favorite brother, so Gawayne is given undeniable incentive to vow vengeance upon Launcelot.[3] From this point on in the *Morte*, it is Gawayne who forces his uncle, King Arthur, to fight with Launcelot, and thus eventually it is Gawayne's anger that causes the kingdom to collapse. By naming Gauwaine as Guenevere's accuser, Morris eliminated unnecessary details and addressed the heart of the matter. Further, in the *Morte*, Gawayne's mother, Margawse, was decapitated as punishment for adultery, so Morris may have cast his Gauwaine in the role of accuser because this character historically realizes "the ramifications of adultery and its punishment" (Silver 197).

Morris's Guenevere responds to Gauwaine's charges by employing an assortment of methods, each involving a degree of doublespeak. Morris may have purposely made Guenevere's defense equivocal because the *Morte* is unclear about the night in question. In his editorial comments, Malory refused to judge the situation and simply noted that his source was vague about what, on this specific occasion, Launcelot did in the Queen's chamber: "For, as the Freynshhe booke seyth, the quene and sir Launcelot were togydirs. And whether they were abed other at other maner of disportis, me lyste nat thereof make no mencion, for love that tyme was nat as love ys nowadayes" (1165; bk. 20, chap. 3). Malory was not so inexact about Launcelot and the Queen's transgression in another situation, when Mellyagaunce kidnaps Gwenyvere. Launcelot rescues the Queen as well as her wounded knights.[4] Under the protection of Launcelot, the group agrees to spend the night in Mellyagaunce's castle, with the wounded knights sleeping just outside Gwenyvere's door. During the night, Launcelot cuts his hand while breaking a bar so that he can enter a window of the Queen's chamber (at her invitation). Malory makes it fairly clear that the two have sexual relations, despite Launcelot's bleeding hand: "Sir Launcelot wente to bedde with the quene and toke no force of hys hurte hand, but toke hys pleasaunce and his lykynge untyll hit was the dawnyng of the day" (1131; bk. 19, chap. 6).

In the morning, after Launcelot has safely departed from the chamber, but before the Queen has risen from her bed, the scoundrel Sir Mellyagaunce forces his way into the room (presumably to view Gwenyvere undressed), pulls back her bed curtains, and discovers blood all over the sheets. Mellyagaunce shouts that Gwenyvere has lain with one of her wounded knights, so Launcelot does not speak untruthfully when he responds by asserting that none of these men were in the Queen's bed. Launcelot's challenge here is much like Guenevere's word play throughout "The Defence."[5]

Indeed, although this character never defends herself in the *Morte*, Morris created a Guenevere who appears to be a seasoned and logical rhetorician. Lawrence Perrine finds Morris's

Guenevere a woman of passion who "defends herself, not logically, but boldly" (240). This argument, while occasionally justifiable, seems untrue overall. With the exception of a few blunders, the Queen's speech is rational throughout--amazingly so when we remember that she is in imminent danger of being consumed by fire in a public spectacle. When Guenevere errs, it may be Morris's way of reminding the reader that the Queen is speaking under duress; she is stalling in an effort to gain more time for Launcelot's arrival.

Although there is a narrator who interrupts three times to explain the Queen's movements or to admire her beauty and bravery, the poem is mostly a dramatic monologue recited by Guenevere and written in *terza rima* form (with the exception of a concluding quatrain). Although the Queen's rhetorical strategy is sometimes annoyingly discursive, Morris probably meant for this to highlight Guenevere's intelligence; each time she alters her argumentative stance, the Queen's keen observation of her audience's reaction is reflected. Guenevere is speaking to the lords of Arthur's kingdom, men she has known for many years, so she changes her style based on their expressions. Also, some of the fragmentation of her discourse can be attributed to those stylistic features: enjambment, abruptness, and colloquial syntax--that Morris apparently borrowed from Browning's dramatic monologues.

After the poem's abrupt, jarring beginning, it is the narrator's comments about the Queen's physical beauty and movements that are most noticeable. Vying simultaneously for a reader's attention are the commentator's words conveying Guenevere's embarrassment. Her hair and brow, though most attractive, are wet with perspiration. The reader's awareness of Guenevere's discomfort throughout the speech is heightened by her gestures; here, the Queen touches her burning cheek, although she walks with her head proudly uplifted. The word "shame" is repeated three times by the narrator, but it is impossible to know if Guenevere's feeling of shame is the ramification of a guilty conscience, or if it is the reaction of a Queen whose conduct has been challenged in her own court; it seems likely that Morris intended for this character, whose arguments alternate between meek protestations and proud denials, to reflect both responses.

Before Guenevere's first argument, involving the "strange choosing cloths" (34), she humbles herself before her audience: [6]

> God wot I ought to say, I have done ill,
> And pray you all forgiveness heartily!
> Because you must be right such great lords--still
>
> (13-15)

Having flattered her listeners, the Queen tries to make these men understand her moral dilemma. To encourage the lords' empathy and to help them see her decision in a larger moral context, Guenevere chooses a male protagonist for her parable. As she discusses this character, Guenevere uses the second person singular pronoun to connect further her audience to the imaginary figure: "Listen, suppose your time were come to die, / And you were quite alone and very weak" (16-17). Guenevere explains that this debilitated man is given an ultimatum by "A great God's angel" (28), and he must decide whether the blue or the red cloth symbolizes spiritual salvation. After a period of anxious debating within himself, the victim realizes that "No man could tell the better of the two" (36). He finally selects the blue fabric because it is "heaven's color" (38), but the angel informs him that this designates eternal hell.

It is obvious that Guenevere intends for the cloths to indicate her own nearly impossible choice between Arthur and Launcelot; however, which color corresponds to which man is difficult for the reader to ascertain, and a case can be built in either direction. Dennis R. Balch in "Guenevere's Fidelity to Arthur in 'The Defence of Guenevere' and 'King Arthur's Tomb'" (1975) finds the preference for the blue cloth to represent Guenevere's acceptance of her marriage bond with Arthur, the Christian King. This was a blind decision, made before Guenevere had ever felt real love (62). Conversely, John Walter Hollow's article, entitled "William Morris and the Judgment of God" (1971), argues that Guenevere "through no fault of her own chose the blue cloth, chose to love Launcelot, only to discover that 'heaven's colour' really represents hell" (447). Indeed, Hollow's reading seems the more likely of the two if we remember that in her next argument, Guenevere again refers to the "choosing cloths" just as she is portraying Launcelot's arrival, and his growing power over her. Guenevere explains that when to decide: "Behold my judges, then the cloths were brought:/ While I was dizzied thus" (80-81). This seems to indicate that the Queen knows that her decision was incorrect, but that she was confused by her "eager body" (77). Also, the ending of Guenevere's first argument includes the idea that her selection proved sinful, for afterwards she wanted to die, but was afraid to die "for what was sown" (45). Choosing Arthur, her husband, would give Guenevere no reason to fear judgment from God, whereas committing adultery with Launcelot could make her fear damnation. Perhaps Morris meant for the reader to be uncertain, thus somewhat sharing the protagonist's confusion. Guenevere's point is that moral confusion is universal on earth, and so her mistake was unavoidable.

Before the beginning of Guenevere's second argument, the narrator comments anew about the Queen's physical state: "And her great eyes began again to fill, / Though still she stood right up, and never shrunk, / But spoke on bravely, glorious lady fair!" (54-56). One may assume that Guenevere's erect posture reflects her pride and innocence. Her tears are appropriate: they usher in her second argument, one that is based solely upon emotional reactions. The Queen met the great Launcelot when she worried that she would be "stone-cold forever" (88). Pleasure was denied Guenevere because she had allowed herself to be "bought / By Arthur's great name and his little love" (82-83). Launcelot brought her joy, so Guenevere argues that God, the creator of human love, wants his children to love and be happy.

Guenevere stresses that she and Launcelot waited and suffered for a very long time before they released themselves into the inevitable consummation of their love. Theirs was no sudden attraction that necessitated immediate or frenzied coupling. The relationship grew more subtly and was not without small obstructions, as Guenevere relates in her analogy of slipping into the sea:

> So day by day it grew, as if one should
>
> Slip slowly down some path worn smooth and even,
> Down to a cool sea on a summer day;

Yet still in slipping was there some small leaven

Of stretched hands catching small stones by the way,
Until one surely reached the sea at last,
And felt strange new joy as the worn head lay

Back, with the hair like sea-weed; yea all past
Sweat of the forehead, dryness of the lips,
Washed utterly out by the dear waves o'ercast

In the lone sea, far off from any ships!
                                        (93-103)

In an archetypal sense, Guenevere allows herself to be submerged in a universal sea of love that washes away her personal consciousness (Stallman 660). This symbolic description of the sexual act may be an avoidance technique on Morris's part, allowing the poet to refrain from writing more erotic verse. It seems more likely, however, that Guenevere intends that the idea of the water of life shall introduce her next argument concerning a springtime rebirth.

In her third section, Guenevere pleads a sort of temporary insanity brought on by her delight in the beauty of the earth as this joy combined with her realization of her own beauty. She convincingly re-creates the atmosphere "of that wild day" (105), explaining that the pleasure she felt in her walled garden drove her nearly mad. Guenevere recalls that in this spring renewal, she and nature shared a new blossoming. The lonely Queen was able to revel in a glorious feeling of freedom. Guenevere now loosens her long hair and spreads her arms wide, encouraging the men watching her to feel, as she did on that day, an innocent appreciation of her body and its natural, undeniable, and uncontrollable sensuousness. Just as her audience is enjoying this display of her charms, Guenevere adroitly introduces Launcelot into her garden paradise scene:

But shortly listen--In that garden fair

Came Launcelot walking; this is true, the kiss

> Wherewith we kissed in meeting that spring day,
> I scarce dare talk of the remember'd bliss,
>
> When both our mouths went wandering in one way,
> And aching sorely, met among the leaves;
> Our hands being left behind strained far away.
>   (132-38)

The Queen's mention of the kiss is an admission of some guilt, despite the indication of paralyzed or abandoned hands. Attempting to recall Gauwaine's specific charge, Guenevere quickly follows with the refrain that refers to Gauwaine as a liar. The Queen intends to remind her listeners that "Whatever happened on through all those years" (143), she and her knight were engaged in innocent chatter on the evening when her chamber was stormed by men who were all too eager to condemn the couple for treason.

Guenevere begins her fourth argument by reminding her listeners that she is their superior under the feudal system. Included here, as well, is an ironic questioning of her own abilities as an actress: "Being such a lady could I weep these tears / If this were true? A great queen such as I / Having sinn'd this way, straight her conscience sears" (145-47). The Queen must feel confident now, for she invites Gauwaine to drop his charges. He trembles and may even consider releasing this beautiful creature on the basis of her position and her testimony. Guenevere, in her excitement and anticipation, speaks again too soon, thus losing her advantage before Gauwaine can forgive her. As though she has suddenly remembered the circumstantial connection, Guenevere tells Gauwaine to "Remember in what grave your mother sleeps" (153). This is the worst possible topic for Guenevere to introduce; in the *Morte* Gawayne's mother, Margawse, is discovered in bed with her lover, Lamorak. Margawse, also a queen, is decapitated as punishment for this transgression by her son Gaherys so that she will not bring further shame to her children (612; bk. 10, chap. 24).[7]

Mentioning this incident is an unfortunate blunder, one that Guenevere worsens by threatening to haunt Gauwaine:

> . . . I pray your pity! let me not scream out
> For ever after, when the shrill winds blow
>
> Through half your castle-locks! let me not shout
> For ever after in the winter night
> When you ride out alone! in battle-rout
>
> Let not my rusting tears make your sword light!
> (158-63)

Gauwaine turns away, any thoughts of leniency erased by this vengeful tirade, and by Guenevere's reminder of Margauses's chastisement for adultery.

Swiftly launching into her next argument, Guenevere addresses the Mellyagraunce affair. Here she is on solid ground because her purity was proven by God when He allowed Launcelot to kill Mellyagraunce in a trial by combat. Refusing to explain outright why there was blood upon her bed, Guenevere implies that Mellyagraunce raped her at knife-point, but that she is too noble to speak about this horror. Guenevere shrewdly links her remembrance of this scene and her fear then that she would be burned for treason with her current situation. The Queen's listeners are thus reminded that she was found innocent before. She could almost feel the fire devour her on the first occasion, and presumably these thoughts are vividly imagined once again.[8] Guenevere reminds her audience of Mellyagraunce's untimely death, a murder sanctified by God, and strongly suggests that the same may happen to them if this second trial continues:

> . . .Yet Mellyagraunce was shent,
> For Mellyagraunce had fought against the Lord;
> Therefore, my lords, take heed lest you be blent
>
> With all this wickedness; say no rash word
> Against me, being so beautiful; my eyes,
> Wept all away to grey, may bring some sword
>
> To drown you in your blood;
> (220-26)

Realizing that by threatening the lords, she may anger them enough to torch her immediately, the Queen changes her tactics yet again in this dizzying array of rhetoric. Guenevere alters the subject by once more flaunting her most effective weapon: her own body. She begins this, her sixth argument, by introducing beautiful parts of herself that have yet gone unmentioned. To distract the men immediately from her ill-contrived menace, Guenevere lures their attention to her breasts--the portion of her anatomy most likely to rapidly attract their consideration away from her previous words. Setting up her next attack, she implores a continuation of this physical scrutiny by demanding that the lords examine her arms, throat, mouth, hands, hair, and brow. Her argument is typically medieval, that physical beauty reflects spiritual goodness:

> . . . will you dare,
> When you have looked a little on my brow,
>
> To say this thing is vile? or will you care
> For any plausible lies of cunning woof,
> When you can see my face with no lie there
>
> For ever? Am I not a gracious proof--
> (236-41)

It is interesting to note that in Tennyson's "Guinevere," published one year after Morris's poem, Arthur's fatal mistake is that he is caught up in just this sort of reasoning. Morris's Guenevere manipulates the premise of her beauty being spiritual, as well, to introduce the possibility that the relationship between Launcelot and herself was one of noncarnal courtly love. Guenevere explains that she asked Launcelot to come to her chamber simply because she was lonely and wanted to talk. In the *Morte* it is clear that Launcelot goes to "speke wyth the quene. . . . and make no taryynge" (1164; bk. 20, chap. 2).

According to Guenevere, courteous Launcelot came to her room because she invited him, attempting temporarily to allay her dark thoughts. She endeavors to evoke her audience's sympathy by relating how she, afraid to be alone, begged Launcelot to visit:

> If you come not, I fear this time I might
> Get thinking over much of times gone by,
> When I was young, and green hope was in sight;
>
> For no man cares now to know why I sigh;
> And no man comes to sing me pleasant songs,
> Nor any brings me the sweet flowers that lie
>
> So thick in the gardens
>   (253-59)

This reiteration of the queen's plea to her knight also serves to remind Guenevere's listeners that the King does not love his wife, and therefore, presumably, Arthur should not mind her accepting the attentions of another man. Still, even with the addition of this implied excuse, Guenevere in her next lines retreats into a posture of innocence. She continues to replay her petition to Launcelot: "therefore one so longs / To see you, Launcelot, that we may be / Like children once again, free from all wrongs / Just for one night" (259-62). Guenevere means to explain her guiltless desire for company, but the inclusion of the last phrase, "Just for one night," seems an inappropriate addition, in that it implies that, on other nights, the two were involved in unchaste activities.

Finally, Guenevere launches into a re-creation of the evening on which she and Launcelot were interrupted by stones thrown at the window.[9] This seventh section begins promisingly enough, and just as it seems that Guenevere will explain Launcelot's feelings, she stops her tale abruptly: "By God! I will not tell you more to-day, / Judge any way you will--what matters it?" (277-78).[10] Guenevere has heard the hoofbeats of Launcelot's roan charger, and so she knows that she will be liberated. Although she does not continue her defense because there is no need, Morris showed, by stopping her speech in midargument, that Guenevere could have continued, possibly indefinitely. The Queen's ample rhetorical skill allowed her to enthrall a group of men (who were likely already worked into that frenzied, blood lust mentality frequently noted at public executions) long enough to ensure her survival.

Morris did not continue the poem to reflect Malory's version of the many knights slaughtered by Launcelot as he slashes his way to Guenevere. The poet concludes his work pleasantly with a romantic line: "The knight who came was Launcelot at good need" (295). Unless a reader knew the scene that follows in the *Morte*, this would seem a happy ending. Had Morris included Launcelot's killing spree and its tragic ramifications (Gawayne's desire for vengeance, Launcelot's war that removes King Arthur from the kingdom, and Mordred's usurpation), he would have risked negating the possibility of his readers feeling sympathetic towards the Queen. As it is, the poem allows an audience to be less judgmental and more understanding of Guenevere's moral confusion. We are able, at least temporarily, to believe in the omnipotence of love. While we may not completely pardon the lovers, Guenevere's plea allows us to commiserate enough to be pleased that her passion will not cause her death. Morris created a powerful figure who seems somehow beyond conventional morality: "Morris's genius is in his refusal to render a smug verdict upon her. His testimony, as well as hers, is to the formidable power of erotic passion which can dissolve all other values in it" (Silver, *Romance*, 25).

Angela Carsoni in "Morris' Guenevere: A Further Note" (1963) finds Guenevere to be akin to figures of Greek tragedy because of the irony of her position: she defies "Gauwaine with words which are at once an admission of guilt and an insistence upon her innocence" (134). While it is impossible to know if Morris intended for his Guenevere to assume this larger, mythic importance, it is evident that "The Defence" does not underscore the principles of conventional morality so favored by Tennyson (and in some respects, Arnold as well). Although it is to be expected that readers will dissect this ambiguous poem for arguments for and against the Queen's innocence, "it should be remembered that Morris was not writing a poem he expected to be 'solved' and may himself have had no consistent interpretation of the character in mind" (Kirchoff 87). Morris's refusal to condemn Guenevere, who is clearly an adultress in his source, might make the poem seem infuriating to a Victorian audience; however, the work's deliberate obscuring of values makes it of the sort modern readers often admire.

"KING ARTHUR'S TOMB"

"King Arthur's Tomb" was suggested to Morris visually by Rossetti and literarily by Malory. Morris briefly owned a Rossetti watercolor called *Arthur's Tomb* (1854) that shows a tormented Launcelot seeking a kiss from a resisting Guenevere. The figure of Launcelot, with facial features said to resemble Morris's, leans over a tomb carved on the top with an image of Arthur (Lang 509). The lovers are surrounded by apple trees, and a coiled snake untwists itself in the grass; thus the Garden of Eden is suggested (Silver, *Romance*, 25, 197).

As noted by David Staines, the poem follows Malory's version of Launcelot and Gwenyvere's last meeting, except that Morris again compressed and simplified some details (444). In the *Morte*'s chapter 21, "The Dolorous Death and Departing," Launcelot and his knights sail to Dover with the intention of joining Arthur's forces against Mordred. When Launcelot discovers that he has arrived too late, he first visits the tomb of Gawayne at Dover Castle before searching for Gwenyvere in Almsburye. If Launcelot sojourns to Arthur's tomb in Glastonbury before he buries Gwenyvere in a nearby plot seven years later, Malory does not mention the pilgrimage. In "King Arthur's Tomb," Guenevere's nunnery is relocated in Glastonbury, at the same site as Arthur's tomb. By devising the lovers' meeting at Arthur's graveside (rather than inside the cloister as the scene is portrayed in the *Morte*), Morris affirmed Rossetti's watercolor interpretation and elevated the situation's bitter irony.

"King Arthur's Tomb" begins with Launcelot's long ride to Glastonbury. He is exasperated by the heat and the steadily slow pace of his horse, but distracts himself by recalling his past with Guenevere. Despite the horror this love has partially caused, Launcelot is still completely devoted to the Queen. Launcelot's memories concentrate mostly upon Guenevere's physical attributes, such as her hair, eyes, feet, hands, mouth, head, and bosom. Not surprisingly, this description culminates in Launcelot's desire to once again touch the Queen. However, his feelings are not merely lustful; love has touched Launcelot so deeply that he equates Guenevere with something akin to Christian spirituality. He remembers Guenevere "smiling like heaven" (27) and imagines

the moon shining "like a star she shed / When she dwelt up in
heaven a while ago, / And ruled all things but God" (64-66).

In the morning, when Launcelot arrives in the town where
his lover dwells, he finally recalls Arthur's death. This thought is
momentarily sobering, but he swiftly becomes "giddy" again,
knowing that he is so close to finding Guenevere after their long
separation. In his fantasies, Launcelot conveniently forgets that
their relationship has caused great destruction, and he ends his long
journey still assuming that Guenevere will return his passion,
despite the loss of her husband, castle, and kingdom. Indeed, had
Launcelot arrived one day earlier, he might have found his queen's
feelings for him unaltered. However, Guenevere, who spent a night
of waiting that was as wretched as Launcelot's, learned during this
time to regard their relationship as sinful:

> This was because
> As she lay last night on her purple bed,
> Wishing for morning, grudging every pause
> Of the palace clocks, until that Launcelot's head
>
> Should lie on her breast, with all her golden hair
> Each side--when suddenly the thing grew drear,
> In morning twilight, when the grey downs bare
> Grew into lumps of sin to Guenevere.
>   (133-40)

Her new awareness of sin disgusts and frightens Guenevere. The
omniscient narrator explains that before the morning, God grants
her salvation. Guenevere now wants to subdue the flesh that she
celebrated earlier in "The Defence," primarily because she
imagines hell as an eternity of enduring churls' insults.

At first, Guenevere's plea for forgiveness from God echoes
her words in "The Defence" when she demanded that the lords
appreciate her physical attractiveness. Guenevere asks God, "Dost
thou reck / That I am beautiful, Lord, even as you / And your dear
Mother?" (168-70). In her confusion, Guenevere thinks of Christ
and Launcelot as rival lovers:

> If even I go to hell, I cannot choose

> But love you, Christ, yea, though I cannot keep
> From loving Launcelot; O Christ! must I lose
> My own heart's love?
>
> (173-76)

Showing that she has chosen God, with a Magdalen gesture, Guenevere kisses the floor, pretending it is Christ's feet.[11] She is now able to weep, a release she dared not enjoy earlier for fear of being observed by her critical attendants. Indeed, as Guenevere lies crying, one of her ladies does interrupt to announce Launcelot's arrival at the King's tomb.

The remainder of the poem echoes the *Morte*'s similar scene, except that Malory's Gwenyvere does not seem interested in Launcelot's salvation; her speech before her attendants is more of a public denunciation of Launcelot's love than an attempt to save his soul:

> Thorow thys same man and me hath al thys warre be wrought, and the deth of the moste nobelest knyghtes of the worlde; for thorow oure love that we have loved togydir is my moste noble lorde slayne. Therefore, sir Launcelot, wyte thou well I am sette in suche a plyght to gete my soule [hele]. And yet I truste, thorow Goddis grace and thorow Hys Passion of Hys woundis wyde, that aftir my deth I may have a syght of the blyss[ed] face of Cryste Jesu, and on Doomesday to sytte on Hys ryght syde; [fo]r as synfull as ever I was, now ar seyntes in hevyn. And there[f]ore, sir Launcelot, I requyre the and beseche the hartily, for all the lo[v]e that ever was betwyxt us, that thou never se me no more in the visayge. And I commaunde the, on Goddis behalff, that thou forsake my company. And to thy kyngedom loke thou turne agayne, and kepe well thy realme frome warre and wrake, for as well as I have loved the heretofore, myne [har]te woll nat serve now to se the; for thorow the and me ys the f[lou]re of kyngis and [knyghtes] destroyed. And therefore [go] thou to thy realme, [an]d there take ye a wyff, and lyff with [hir wyth] joy and blys. [A]nd I pray the hartely to pray for me [to] the Everlastynge Lorde [tha]t I may amende my mysselyvyng. (1252; bk. 21, chap. 9)

Although Gwenyvere has abandoned the diction of courtly love, Launcelot still responds in his old way:

> "Now, my swete madame," seyde sir Launcelot, "wolde ye that I shuld turne agayne unto my contrey and therto wedde a lady? Nay, madame, wyte you well that shall I never do, for I shall never be so false unto you of that I have promysed." (1252-53; bk. 21, chap. 9)

Next, Launcelot claims that because Gwenyvere has given her life to God, he will do the same. Gwenyvere does not believe that he is capable of foregoing earthly pleasures, and her skepticism seems justified by his parting request: "Wherfore, madame, I praye you kysse me, and never no more" (1253; bk. 21, chap. 10). The Queen refuses to grant Launcelot one last kiss, and this emotional moment of rejection causes both to swoon repeatedly. Launcelot does not see Gwenyvere again until he returns as a priest, many years later, to perform her burial mass.

In Morris's poem, Guenevere's words to Launcelot are equally harsh, but because the reader is made to understand both her psychological turmoil and her intention to shock Launcelot into repentance, Guenevere here seems much kinder than she does in the *Morte*. In the poem Guenevere intends to free Launcelot from his earthly love. He is morally obtuse, so she must be deliberately cruel, forcing him to abandon his animal nature and, thus, repaying him for the many times he saved her earthly life. When the exhausted Launcelot, unaware that he rests on the tomb of Arthur, looks up to see his love, she is not dressed in the cheerful green he remembers, but in stark black. Because Guenevere looks different and her first words are in praise of her husband, Launcelot fears that she is either insane or an impostor. Guenevere responds, "I am not mad, but I am sick; they cling, / God's curses, unto such as I am; not / Ever again shall we twine arms and lips" (195-97). Launcelot, still uncertain of her sanity, begs repeatedly for a kiss. In a moment of weakness, Guenevere seeks heavenly strength to deny Launcelot and to complete her task: "Christ! my hot lips are very near his brow, / Help me to save his soul!" (207-8).

Guenevere, apparently granted heavenly inspiration, returns to her work with a perfect attack that is devoid of the denials of

adultery found in "The Defence." Guenevere begins here to liken
Launcelot to a tempting snake, an analogy she continues later, and
one that recalls Rossetti's painting. She sarcastically suggests that
they make love upon the tomb:

> Across my husband's head, fair Launcelot!
> Fair serpent mark'd with V upon the head!
> This thing we did while yet he was alive,
> Why not, O twisting knight, now he is dead?
>   (209-12)

Next, as Guenevere begins to describe the first time she
met Launcelot, he interrupts, "Will she lie now, Lord God?" (221).
Launcelot's meaning is unclear, but he may be wondering if
Guenevere will continue to deny her attraction to him, even back to
their introduction, thus placing the blame for their adultery on him.
In the following section, it seems that Launcelot has anticipated
her mood correctly; the Queen momentarily blames both Arthur
and Launcelot for the transgression she so recently confessed to
God.

Guenevere continues to reproach Launcelot until she
remembers her past unkindness to her attendants, caused by her
obsession with her lover, and asks their forgiveness:

> Alas, my maids, you loved not overmuch
> Queen Guenevere, uncertain as sunshine
> In March; forgive me! for my sin being such,
> About my whole life, all my deeds did twine,
>
> Made me quite wicked.
>   (297-301)

Remembering her past testiness, the Queen is humbled enough to
recollect other events more correctly. Earlier, Guenevere
complained that in the early days of her affair, she had felt a
discomfort at being unable to "live a righteous life" (263). Now,
however, the Queen realizes that she never cared about her soul,
and she recalls daydreaming during the priest's sermons at daily
mass.

Perhaps because Launcelot's comments thus far have indicated his continuing adherence to the thoroughly anachronistic concept of courtly love, Guenevere begins to recall jousts where the knights fought for the honor of their ladies (rather than God). These memories prove too intense, and Guenevere, crying, sinks to the ground. The slow-witted Launcelot still does not realize that Guenevere is completely renouncing him; thinking that he has found the perfect romantic solution, Launcelot suggests that Guenevere kill him now and later reclaim him as her heavenly lover. Guenevere, either because she realizes that her rhetoric thus far has been useless, or because she is finally disgusted by Launcelot's misunderstanding of her desire to be freed from him, launches her most vehement attack:

> Here let me tell you what a knight you are,
> O sword and shield of Arthur! you are found
> A crooked sword, I think, that leaves a scar
>
> On the bearer's arm, so he thinks it straight,
> Twisted Malay's crease beautiful blue-grey,
> Poison'd with sweet fruit; as he found too late,
> My husband Arthur, on some bitter day!
>
> . . .
>
> Banner, and sword, and shield, you dare not pray to die,
> Lest you meet Arthur in the other world,
> And, knowing who you are, he pass you by,
> Taking short turns that he may watch you curl'd
>
> Body and face and limbs in agony,
> Lest he weep presently and go away,
> Saying, "I loved him once," with a sad sigh.
> (370-76, 381-87)

These cruel words cause Launcelot to fall. Guenevere, believing that she has killed him, prays for her own death.[12] Guenevere's last

words reflect her belief that by denying Launcelot one last kiss, she
has behaved correctly.

Launcelot, awakening from his swoon, discovers blood
dripping from his head and hands where he has cut them on stones.
These stigmatic wounds (Stallman 669) and the sacring bell
Launcelot hears indicate his religious conversion. In the *Morte*,
Launcelot also awakens to a bell; then he attends a mass officiated
by the Bishop of Canterbury and afterward begs the Bishop to
make him a brother. Launcelot stays at the chapel and eventually
becomes a priest. Clearly, although some critics suggest that the
bell is Guenevere's death toll (Silver, *Romance*, 25; Oberg 157;
Carley 14), Morris uses the bell in "King Arthur's Tomb," as
Malory did in the *Morte*, to indicate Launcelot's new spiritual
grace and to foreshadow his life as a monk.

In "King Arthur's Tomb," Morris reversed the characters
of Launcelot and Guenevere from what they appeared to be in
"The Defence of Guenevere." The defiant Queen, who spoke in
half-truths while waiting to be rescued is transformed into a
repentant woman offering salvation to her knight. Launcelot, the
romantic hero who arrived at the perfect moment to save his lady,
becomes a vulnerable, jilted lover writhing under Guenevere's
constant reproaches. Morris did not seem to feel that Launcelot and
Guenevere's adulterous amour should have been entirely avoided.
The reader is aware that the lovers did repent, but their suffering is
limited to one night and part of a day. Both the Queen and her
knight gain Christian salvation--possibly because their adulterous
relationship became a catalyst for repentance.

Morris is consistently true to the spirit, if not the letter, of
the *Morte*. However, his adherence to Malory's outcome seems too
rushed in "King Arthur's Tomb" to be believable; it seems as
though the poet was uncomfortable with this conclusion. Perhaps
this strained feeling is indicative of Morris's growing need to allow
sensuousness to reign supreme:

> That Arthur and Christian asceticism not only can but must,
> within the context of Arthurian legend, overcome
> Launcelot and the sensuous life he represents may be one
> reason why Morris did not utilize Arthurian material in a
> major way during his poetic career. Perhaps he realized that

the Arthurian legends embodied a system of values contrary to the values he himself was developing which would depend upon the central importance of the individual sensual experience rather than a denial of man's animal nature. (Balch 70)

Morris continued in his next poem to examine this difference between celestial and earthly love.

"SIR GALAHAD: A CHRISTMAS MYSTERY"

In "Sir Galahad, a Christmas Mystery" and "The Chapel in Lyoness," the final two purely Arthurian poems of Morris's 1858 volume, Galahad replaces Guenevere as the central figure. As an undergraduate at Oxford, Morris wrote a letter to his friend "Crom" (Cormell Price), announcing his intention to found a brotherhood with Sir Galahad as the brotherhood's patron saint or monastic ideal. Morris asked "Crom" to memorize Tennyson's 1842 version of "Morte d'Arthur" so that "Crom" too could become a member of the brotherhood, whose purpose was to bring Christianity and Christian charity to the poor areas of London. Eventually, Morris became disillusioned with the idea of the fraternity as well as entering the church, but his interest in Galahad remained (Harrison and Waters 11-20).

The protagonist of "Sir Galahad, a Christmas Mystery," on the longest eve of the year, the dark night of his soul, is plagued by feelings of self-pity and doubt. Galahad worries that celestial love cannot replace the experiences of earthly love. Morris was again intent upon analyzing an Arthurian character's possible psychological turmoil, and since Malory's Galahad never expresses doubt, this incident was largely created by the poet.[13] An emphasis upon Galahad's pain and loneliness, rather than his joy and redemption, combines with the poem's stark conclusion to suggest the frustration caused by an ascetic ideal. Indeed, "Morris makes clear, long before Tennyson's bitter treatment of 'The Holy Grail,' that the pursuit of a purely spiritual goal can bring destruction" (Silver 31). We do not see Galahad's ultimate success and are left with the knowledge that Sir Lionel and Sir Gauwaine are shamed, Sir Lauvaine is wounded, and Sir Dinadan is dead.

The poem begins with the description of a stark, cold, winter night, an atmosphere Morris uses to suggest Galahad's spirituality. This replaces the burning heat that indicated the passion of the characters in "The Defence of Guenevere" and "King Arthur's Tomb." After he has been sitting inside the chapel for six hours, Galahad begins to express his thoughts.[14] Galahad's interior monologue (later the form shifts to dramatic action) begins with the complaint that he has no courtly lover, and therefore he cannot entertain or warm himself during his solitary wandering with fantasies about a woman. With Galahad's first words, the reader is forced to realize that this is not the stoic and chaste Red Cross Knight of the *Morte* or of the French vulgate *Quest*.

Half-asleep, Galahad contrasts his loveless life with the contentment of Palomydes, who follows the Questing Beast to win Iseult of Cornwall's attention. It matters not that Iseult, smitten by Tristram, will never return Palomydes's affection:

> For unto such a man love-sorrow is
> So dear a thing unto his constant heart,
> That even if he never win one kiss,
> Or touch from Iseult, it will never part.
>
> And he will never know her to be worse
> Than in his happiest dreams he thinks she is:
> Good knight and faithful, you have 'scaped the curse
> In wonderful-wise; you have great store of bliss.
>
> (33-40)

The phrase "'scaped the curse" probably refers to the advantages of Palomydes's unconsummated relationship with Iseult, a love that is not sinful because it is not adulterous. Still, Galahad is also jealous of Launcelot's less innocent love for Guenevere. The chaste knight laments that he rides about without the same type of comforting thoughts that dispel his father's loneliness:

> Yea, what if Father Launcelot ride out,
> Can he not think of Guenevere's arms, round,

> Warm and lithe, about his neck, and shout
> Till all the place grows joyful with sound?
>
> (41-44)

Lest we imagine that Galahad desires physical intercourse with a woman, Morris swiftly altered the direction of the knight's complaint. Galahad suffers less from sexual frustration than from the knowledge that his death will go unmourned. Imagining that he will be found dead in the snow, wrapped in his own arms, Galahad continues his reverie, grieving that no maid will lament by his tomb. Galahad fancies that the people who discover his corpse will say, "This Galahad / If he had lived had been a right good knight; / Ah! poor chaste body!" (53-55), but still they will enjoy, that very evening, with no further thoughts of his death, the songs of gay minstrels. With his self-pity now at its most fevered point, Galahad recalls a kiss he once witnessed between another knight and his lady. This memory lingers and chokes Galahad, because, like him, this knight was departing to search for the Sangreal.

Earlier, Galahad explained that these hellish thoughts began as he "look'd down on the floor, / Between my feet" (7-8). This unholy meditation ends when, "With sleepy face bent to the chapel floor" (77), Galahad hears a sharp bell. A visitation from Christ, which the ringing bell announces, forces the knight to look heavenward. Galahad, for the first time in his life, feels "what a thing was perfect dread" (92) and waits to be reprimanded for his doubt. But Christ speaks gently to the cowering knight:

> Rise up, and look and listen, Galahad,
> Good knight of God, for you will see no frown
> Upon my face; I come to make you glad.
>
> For that you say that you are all alone,
> I will be with you always, and fear not
> You are uncared for, though no maiden moan
> Above your empty tomb.
>
> (94-100)

After Christ explains that he loves Galahad, he foretells that Launcelot will soon become his servant. Christ says that although

Launcelot is now sustained by his love for Guenevere, this immoral, adulterous union causes Him grief:

> He is just what You know, O Galahad,
> This love is happy even as you say,
> But would you for a little time be glad,
> To make *me* sorry long day after day?
>
> Her warm arms round his neck half throttle Me,
> The hot love-tears burn deep like spots of lead,
> Yea, and the years pass quick: right dismally
> Will Launcelot at one time hang his head.
>
> (105-12)

Further, Christ calls the love of Palomydes "weary work" (118) because it relies on "What chances may betide" (120); Palomydes strives to seem better than he is in actuality only to impress a woman who has no interest in him. This sexual love, even if obtained, will decay with old age. Christ assures Galahad that divine love endures eternally, so the chaste knight is lucky that no lust blinds him on earth.

Galahad falls to the ground and is alone when he looks up again. The bell sounds once more, ushering in two angels and four female saints, who carry a bed for Galahad to rest upon. [15] In the morning, Galahad is awakened by these same six figures and urged by them to find the Sangreal. Here Morris resorts to the *Morte*'s chapter 15 for the story about "the wondrous ship wherein / The spindles of King Solomon are laid, / And the sword that no man draweth without sin / But if he be most pure" (157-60).

Galahad will no longer be alone on his quest because Sir Bors, Sir Percival, and Sir Percival's sister (this nun, although her role is significant, is also unnamed in the *Morte*) arrive to join the search. Sir Bors utters the poem's last lines, words conveying an abrupt change in mood. In the *Morte*, the Grail quest causes the collapse of the Round Table fellowship. Morris indicated this breakdown with Bors's wastelandic speech about the knights who are dead or shamed. Bors explains that although he has glimpsed the great light of the Grail as the holy vessel shone while he was passing through the woods, the adventure has been futile for most of the questers: "Everywhere / The knights come foil'd from the great quest, in vain: / In vain they struggle for the vision fair" (198-200). Although Galahad was granted a beatific vision, Morris, by concluding with a description of the hellish fates that befall other seekers of the Grail, emphasized the destruction caused by this quest. Christ's moving words, indicating the superiority of celibacy, may be the key to understanding the other knights' failures.

In the *Morte*, it is Galahad's virginity that allows his triumph. Also, Galahad's ability to retrieve the Grail and remove it to the spiritual city depends upon his perfect lineage: as the son of Launcelot, Galahad inherits the best qualities of knightly prowess; as the child of Elayne, and, therefore, a descendent of Joseph of Arimathea (who is called, in some medieval romances, the Virgin Mary's uncle), Galahad inherits great spiritual power. In the *Morte*, the Grail appears because Galahad sits in the Sege Perillous; although the other knights see the vessel as well, the quest is Galahad's because the Grail appeared following his arrival, and because his lineage and his celibacy make him the best candidate. As Morris indicated, the other knights are doomed to failure or death. No matter how hard they strive, these knights, who have experienced physical--possibly immoral--love, will never touch the Grail.

"THE CHAPEL IN LYONESS"

Only 92 lines long, "The Chapel in Lyoness" is Morris's shortest Arthurian poem. This concise dramatic episode, first published separately in the September 1856 issue of the *Oxford and Cambridge Magazine,* employs three speakers, Sir Ozana le Cure Hardy, Sir Galahad, and Sir Bors de Ganys, who narrate the story disjunctively, with little personal interaction. Although these characters appear in the *Morte,* Morris created a scene for the figures that is not from medieval romance.

As the poem opens, Ozana lies in the chancel of a deserted chapel, wounded and in delirium. The words "no man any blood could spy" (7) indicate that Ozana's wound is of the spiritual sort, like that of the maimed king in the Percival romances (Silver 31).

Ozana's death-in-life state may be the result of his "hope to rejoin his dead mistress" (L. Stevenson 142), but the evidence is not conclusive; Ozana complains that "the truncheon of a spear" (8) is lodged deep within his breast. The wounded knight, unable to move, speak, cry, or sleep, appears to be in a coma and imagines himself alone.

Galahad has been by Ozana's side, keeping vigil by the deathbed, as Ozana remained in a speechless trance "from Christmas Eve to Whit-Sunday" (2).[16] As Curtis Dahl discusses in "Morris's 'The Chapel in Lyoness': An Interpretation" (1954), Morris, by including Ozana and Galahad in the same poem, mixes two distinct groups of legends from the *Morte* (484). Indeed, Malory did not ever present these two knights together. Ozana, never shown as a knight of great stature, is usually named only as among a group of knights who are either beaten in tournaments or captured in battle. "A second-rate knight," Ozana is an "ordinary, unheroic man," the type of knight who is habitually defeated and must be rescued (Dahl 485). Malory does not name Ozana as one of the Grail seekers, whereas this quest was, of course, the most important event in the lives of Galahad and Bors.

Although Galahad and Ozana do not meet in the *Morte,* Malory includes specific instances in which Galahad performs a service of the type Morris relates in this poem. In Book 17 of the *Morte,* Galahad, a Christ substitute, eases three men peacefully into death. One of these men reminds Galahad, "Much ar ye beholde to thanke God which hath gyven you a good owre, that ye may draw oute the soulis of erthely payne and to putte them into the joyes of Paradyse" (1026; bk. 17, chap. 18).

In "The Chapel in Lyoness," Galahad tries to rouse Ozana by singing; when this does not work, Galahad is able to revive Ozana briefly by placing a rose, sprinkled with water, across the dying man's lips. Ozana smiles and holds up a bit of golden hair, which he then presses to his wounded breast. Sir Bors enters the chapel just as Galahad stoops to give Ozana the kiss of peace. After asking Christ's help and acknowledging that his "life went wrong" (74), Ozana reports, "Now I begin to fathom it" (79), referring to his earlier remark, possibly concerning his confusion about death and salvation: "Ah me, I cannot fathom it" (33). Ozana dies, and Bors explains that Galahad sits staring as though in a trance.

The most interesting part of this poem is the last lines, spoken by Galahad:

> Ozana, shall I pray for thee?
> Her cheek is laid to thine;
> No long time hence, also I see
> Thy wasted fingers twine
>
> Within the tresses of her hair
> That shineth gloriously,
> Thinly outspread in the clear air
> Against the jasper sea.
>   (85-92)

In his vision, Galahad sees Ozana reunited with the mysterious, fair lady. Thus "The Chapel in Lyoness" modifies Galahad's earlier renunciation of earthly love by "portraying his sympathy for the dying lover Ozana and by attributing to him a vision that is not of the Holy Grail, but of a reunion of lovers in Heaven, much like that of Rossetti's 'The Blessed Damozel'" (L. Stevenson 142). Indeed, Morris may have borrowed this mixture of spirit and flesh from Rossetti, but "The Chapel in Lyoness" adds "much more religious mystery" (Kirchoff 101). Read as the conclusion to Morris's Arthurian group, this poem, with its sensual reunion of lovers after death, does little to resolve the paradoxes of sexual experience that the poet seemed intent upon analyzing.

CONCLUSION

Overall, Morris's Arthurian poems reflect the *Liebestöd* motif later elaborated in Wagner's *Tristan und Isolde*: entanglement in an immoral love destroys, with both togetherness and separation conjuring a desire for release through death. Morris shows that the wish for a conclusion to earthly suffering ushers in a host of new concerns about the afterlife. In Morris's first three Arthurian poems, heavenly grace is granted only to those who

renounce earthly, passionate love.   Strangely, Ozana, of "The
Chapel in Lyoness," dies still symbolically clinging to his lover
(her hair), yet he is reunited with her in Galahad's vision. Perhaps
Ozana gained salvation through his confession concerning his
sinful life and his dying plea for God's help. If this last poem
reflects Morris's idea of paradise, he probably also imagined a
heavenly reconciliation for Launcelot and Guenevere. In this
scheme of things, with a repentant death allowing for the return in
heaven of a former love, Galahad's frustrating, chaste life seems all
for nought.

Morris's Arthurian poems reflect characters experiencing
feelings of vacillation between sensual self-indulgence and
spiritual puritanism. The poet seems to have been obsessed with
the theme of immoral sexual desire and the guilt that accompanies
it. The protagonists' problems largely remain unsolved, possibly
suggesting Morris's understanding of the futility involved in
opposing earthly to heavenly love. Perhaps Morris never intended
to resolve this issue, but was more concerned with "the dramatic
depiction of personality in the manner of Browning" (Stallman
657).

Morris did not write about Arthurian legends again, but his
later work suggests that the complications versified in these four
poems were never entirely resolved in his thoughts. Arthurian
material did later become a part of Morris's speeches concerning
political revolution:

> His early attachment to King Arthur had led him irresistibly
> to Karl Marx. The Round Table was a preparation for
> communism--indeed a sort of communism in itself--for he
> contrasted to his lecture audiences the knightly hall in
> which the workers might banquet together with the misery
> of their single rooms in mean tenements. (Gaunt 227)

Further, Morris's understanding that the Grail Quest destroyed the
Round Table probably combined with his knowledge of Marx's
view of oppressive religion to produce the thought that Christianity
destroys brotherhood. Some critics think of Morris as a pagan; if
he was devoid of Christian spirituality, it may be because Morris

was unable to understand why sexual love could not coalesce with divine love.

NOTES

1. Although we never actually hear Gauwaine's accusation in "The Defence," it can be inferred from the poem's content that it is similar to Aggravyne's in the *Morte*, except that it is aimed at Guencvere rather than Launcelot. In the *Morte* it is clear that Arthur already is aware of the amour between his wife and his best friend; the king would prefer not to listen to Aggravayne's accusation:

> We know all that Sir Launcelot holdith youre quene, and hath done longe; and we be your syster sunnes, we may suffir hit no lenger. And all we wote that ye shulde be above sir Launcelot, and ye ar the kynge that made hym. knyght, and therefore we woll preve hit that he is a traytoure to youre person. (1163; bk. 20. chap. 2)

All blame here is directed at Launcelot rather than Gwenyvere; however, when Launcelot escapes, the king decides to punish his wife. Launcclot feels that this sudden transference of blame is a malicious reaction intended to torture him:

> For thes knyghtes were sente by kynge Arthur to betray me, and therefore the kyng woll in thys hete and malice jouge the quene unto brennyng, and that may not I suffir that she shulde be brente for my sake. For and I may be harde and suffirde and so takyn, I woll feyght for the quene, that she ys a trew lady untyll her lorde. But the kynge in hys hete, I drede, woll not take me as I ought to be takyn. (1171; bk. 20, chap. 5)

2. Gawayne is unable to move Arthur with this plea for Gwenyvere's innocence, so he begins to weep heavily. This emotional reaction is typical among the figures of medieval romance, who frequently cry or swoon when they are surprised, disappointed, or embarrassed. A modern reader is likely to be amazed at the frequency with which daring, hardy young knights lapse into such "unmasculine" behavior. While female characters do behave in similarly dramatic ways, their reactions are less noticeable because so few fully developed characters arc women. Malory, who depends upon showing rather than telling, uses weeping and fainting in a wide variety of situations to reflect acute sentiment. Less violent circumstances evoke blushes, the reaction favored by Morris's Guenevere.

3. In his sorrow and anger, Gawayne never considers that Gareth and Launcelot were best friends, or that Gareth's death was clearly an accident.

4. This episode comes from Chrétien's *Lancelot* (c. 1179), but in the French story Launcelot's devotion to the Queen seems ridiculous. Malory gives Launcelot heroic status here and throughout the *Morte*.

5. Malory uses this same type of twisting of the truth earlier when Isode purposely trips over Trystran, who is disguised as a beggar, and then tells King Marke that she has never been touched by any man, except for him and the beggar (Carley 9).

6. This study which aims to thoroughly clarify Guenevere's defense of her illicit love affair, is indebted to Robert Stallman's article "The Lover's Progress: An Investigation of William Morris' 'The Defence of Guenevere' and 'King Arthur's Tomb'" (1975). Stallman divides "The Defence" into seven separate arguments, and although his particular assessment of each section is not reiterated in this chapter, it is his divisions that are employed here. Among the relatively few explications of this poem, Stallman's article is the only one that so conveniently outlines the work.

7. Morris incorrectly named Agravaine, another of Margawse's sons, as the murderer.

8. Meredith B. Raymond concludes that Morris used words reflecting heat to show continuity between "The Defence of Guenevere" and "King Arthur's Tomb": "the heat of the stake, of hot lips, of Guenevere's cheek, of the August day, and the heat of passion, shame, and madness" (215).

9. Robert L, Stallman notes that "the stones thrown at the chamber windows remind us of the Biblical cure for adultery" (664).

10. James P. Carley finds that, with this refusal to speak further, Guenevere reminds one of Shakespeare's Iago (11).

11. Because Guenevere is lying face downward on the floor, this scene is like the one in "Guinevere" of the *Idylls*, except that Tennyson's character grovels before Arthur rather than God.

12. Carol Silver notes that this reflects the *Liebestöd* motif, wherein the tragic nature of an immoral love transforms into a death wish (127).

13. In the *Morte*, Galahad does see "Jesu Cryste bledynge all opynly," but this meeting is not prompted by a doubting knight. Christ appears to grant Galahad a vision of the slightly masked grail and thus encourage the quest:

> "Thys ys," seyde He, "the holy dysshe wherein I ete the lambe on Estir Day, and now hast thou sene that thou moste desired to se. But yet hast thou nay sene hit so opynly as thou shalt se hit in the cité of Sarras, in the spirituall paleyse. Therefore

thou must go hense and beare with thys holy vessell, for this
nyght hit shall departe frome the realme of Logrus, and hit
shall nevermore be sene here. And knowyst thou wherefore?
For he ys nat served nother worshipped to hys ryght by hem of
thys londe, for they be turned to evyll lyvyng, and therefore I
shall disherite them of the honoure whych I have done them.
And therefore go ye three [to-morne] unto the see, where ye
shall fynde youre shippe redy, and with you take the swerde
with the stronge gurdils, and no mo with you but sir Percivale
and sir Bors." (1030; bk. 17, chap. 20)

14. Galahad's mention that he came to the chapel "six hours ago" (3)
makes his lament an implicit equivalent with Christ's passion (leading up to his
cry from the Cross: "My God, My God, why hast thou forsaken me?"); "at the
time of the Crucifixion 'from the sixth hour there was darkness over all the land
until the ninth hour'" (Carley 17).

15. The startling change here from interior monologue to dramatic
action and the introduction of angels accompanied by saints may explain
Morris's use of the word "mystery" in the poem's title. However, if Morris, as
seems likely given the similarities, intended to capture the style of medieval
plays, the poem would be more aptly named "Sir Galahad, a Christmas
Miracle." Medieval miracle plays often dealt with the nonscriptural legends of
saints, whereas the content of medieval mystery plays is usually biblical:

They [mystery plays] seem to have developed around three
nuclei which presented the whole scheme of salvation: Old Testament
plays dealing with such events as the Creation, the fallen angels, the
fall of Adam and Eve, the death of Abel, and the sacrifice of Isaac, and
the Prophet plays, which prepared for (2) the New Testament plays
dealing with the birth of Christ-the Annunciation, the birth, the visit of
the wise men, the shepherds, and the visit to the temple; and (3) the
Death and Resurrection plays-entry into Jerusalem, the betrayal by
Jesus, trial and crucifixion, lamentation of Mary, sepulchre scenes, the
resurrection, appearances to disciples, Pentecost, and sometimes the
Day of Judgement. (Holman and Harmon 315)

Further, although "A Christmas Morality" would sound awkward,
Morris could have used this title because the medieval moralities, such as
Everyman (1500), "were plays of a didactic, ethical nature" (Garbáty 907);
however, the characters of these plays personified human traits, while Morris's
characters do not reflect vices and virtues. It is interesting that Christ appears in
"Sir Galahad, a Christmas Mystery," and that God is among the *Dramatis
Personae* of *Everyman*.

16. Curtis Dahl reads the poem as a "spiritual drama" and finds that this
period of time has biblical connotations as it symbolically encompasses the

whole of the life of Christ, from his birth through his Passion to the descent of the Holy Spirit on his Disciples at Pentecost. It is at Pentecost, then, the day on which wonders frequently happened at Arthur's court and on which the Holy Grail had originally appeared, that the poem's action takes place (488).

Chapter 5

Algernon Swinburne

The underlying characteristics of Algernon Swinburne's Arthurian poetry are similar to those found in his other works. Although many of his poems are stylistically innovative, what are most striking in his works, as opposed to those of other Victorian Arthurian poets, are ideological views that constitute a rebellion against "the limited and limiting moral, political, and religious values of his own historical era" (A. Harrison 2). Apparently attempting to reflect his opinions in a manner less offensive to Victorian readers, Swinburne often adopted a poetic stance outside his historical moment.

Having spent many childhood hours examining medieval manuscripts in the library of his uncle (the Earl of Ashburnham), Swinburne was a medieval scholar well before he met Rossetti and Morris at Oxford. The poet had studied enough to understand the concepts of medieval Christianity, yet as an avowed and iconoclastic atheist, he consistently developed medieval characters who are misguided in their adherence to Christian values or who trust in Love and Fate as supreme deities.

Although Swinburne wrote on many medieval topics, only seven of his poems are purely Arthurian. Rather than compose an entire Arthurian cycle like Tennyson, Swinburne concentrated on the Arthurian characters and situations that could best reflect his particular philosophy: "If he had planned a complete Arthurian cycle, he probably abandoned the idea because much of the material clearly did not suit his artistic taste or his temperament. For instance, it is doubtful that a repentant Lancelot or Guinevere or a righteous Galahad would have appealed to his sensibilities" (Cochran, "Arthuriana" 66). The love of Tristram and Iseult, traditionally depicted in medieval works as the result of fate, with predetermined fortune symbolized in the love potion, is a narrative through which Swinburne could extol heroic individuals who accept their destiny despite the laws of God and man. The story of Balen, a knight who consistently acts in socially unacceptable ways that he nonetheless considers correct, as well as the knight who is doomed by fate to cause grief in every situation, is another appropriate vehicle for Swinburne's fatalistic vision. Similarly, when Swinburne focused on such Arthurian characters as Arthur, Lancelot, and Ban, he chose only those portions of their lives that exposed the characters' acceptance of Fate, Love, or the laws of nature.

Particularly in his mature works, the poet rarely deviated from the sources' medieval plots, except occasionally to tighten the structure, because he chose to develop only those stories that could be enhanced by the addition of philosophic sections reflecting his own beliefs. Swinburne responded to and amplified Arthurian material for some four decades; his thematic concerns worked well in the tragedies of Camelot, just as he had used them in various Hellenic narratives.[1]

Swinburne's Arthuriana can be conveniently divided into three phases: the juvenilia or "practice poems" (Cochran, "Arthuriana" 65) composed between 1857 and 1859, the masterwork *Tristram of Lyonesse* (1882), and the relatively late piece, *The Tale of Balen* (1896). David Staines suggests in his article "Swinburne's Arthurian World" (1978) that of "all of the Victorian writers who turned to the Arthurian legend for artistic inspiration, only Alfred Tennyson made a larger contribution than Swinburne to the Arthurian renaissance" (53).

THE EARLY WORKS

Swinburne arrived as an undergraduate at Oxford not only with a knowledge of the many fine illuminated manuscripts owned by his uncle, but also with a special appreciation for Sir Thomas Malory. The young man quickly became a disciple of Rossetti and Morris, who thought that they were offering "Swinburne his Arthurian baptism by providing him with the Pre-Raphaelite method of recreating the medieval world" (Staines "Swinburne" 59). But Swinburne appears to have read medieval literature more enthusiastically and extensively, "to have studied it more thoughtfully, and to have retained more of what he read than either Morris or Rossetti" (A. Harrison 6). Between 1857 and 1859, Swinburne composed five short Arthurian poems (some were fragments), nearly all written in response to Morris's Arthurian works that were composed during the same period and published in *The Defence of Guenevere and Other Poems* (1859). Swinburne's early Arthurian works are "Queen Yseult" (1857-58), "King Ban" (1857), "The Day before the Trial" (1857-58), "Lancelot" (1858), and "Joyeuse Garde" (1859).

Although Swinburne planned it in ten cantos, "Queen Yseult" remains an unfinished work in six cantos of irregular iambic tetrameter rhyming tercets. The first canto appeared in a volume of *Undergraduate Papers* in 1857, but the entire poem was not published until 1918. While Swinburne seems to have known the *Tristan* of Béroul and other French versions of the story from a compilation by Francisque Michel, he relied mostly on Sir Walter Scott's 1804 edition of the Middle English a *Sir Tristrem* by Thomas of Ercildoune. Swinburne borrowed some details from Malory, and he was familiar with Arnold's "Tristram and Iseult" (1852), although "Queen Yseult" concerns the lovers in their early period and ends long before the portion of the story related by Arnold.

Swinburne arrived at Balliol in January of 1856, and by November 1, 1857, he had met Morris, who was painting the story of Tristram and Iseult on the Oxford Union walls. Morris's enthusiasm apparently rekindled Swinburne's interest in the tale, but the first result was a slavish, "all-too-close imitation" of Morris's early unpublished work, rather than of those poems included in *The Defence of Guenevere and Other Poems* that inspired Swinburne's other short Arthurian poems (Henderson "Swinburne" 30).[2] "Queen Yseult"'s graphic, sensuous depictions of scenery and characters render it much more Pre-Raphaelite than medieval in tone:

> The unfinished poem is less a recreation of the legends than a simplification of the plot which becomes the basis for a distinctly Pre-Raphaelite portrait of Yseult. Source material serves the same function here that Malory serves for Morris' Arthurian poetry; it is only the suggestion for a Pre-Raphaelite study of a passionate woman and the tragic consequences of her love. (Staines, "Swinburne" 55)

Swinburne deliberately ignored much of the action and adventure described in *Sir Tristrem* and other sources, characteristically choosing instead to focus upon the love story of Tristram and Yseult. While "Queen Yseult"'s plot closely follows the outline of the medieval romance, Swinburne frequently deviates for extended, aesthetic descriptions that make his poem seem like a Pre-Raphaelite painting in words. Queen Yseult is repeatedly represented by "her golden hair corn-ripe" (canto I 339). She is, in fact, indistinguishable from her tresses and is referred to as "Yseult queen, the hair of gold" (I 333). Her hair "flowed and glowed" (195) in canto 2, but becomes almost another character by the poem's end when the "weeping" (IV 80) hair moves the saints to pity the Queen. Elisabeth G. Gitter, in "The Power of Women's Hair in the Victorian Imagination" (1984), notes that golden hair in Swinburne's works is rarely innocent and generally gains an active, aggressive, and erotic life of its own (952).[3]

Following a four-stanza introduction, the poem begins by describing another fair-haired woman, Tristram's mother Blauncheflour, whose great love for Roland causes her to follow him to Ermonie. The travel is difficult, but Blauncheflour, with typical courtly ethos, does not regret her decision to risk everything for love any more than her son does later:

> "Lo!" she said, "I lady free
> Took this man for lord of me
> Where the crowned saints might see."
>   (I 22-24)

Most of the first canto is devoted to the love of Tristram's parents, their sad deaths, their son's revenge upon Moronde for those deaths, and the building of a tomb in their honor. The faithful and noble relationship of Blauncheflour and Roland sets an example for Tristram and foreshadows his doom. At the canto's conclusion, Tristram arrives in Cornwall, is acknowledged by his uncle, King Mark, and is sent to capture the Irish Yseult's heart so that she may become Mark's queen.

Unlike his later work *Tristram of Lyonesse*, "Queen Yseult" demonstrates Swinburne's inattention to details found in earlier versions of the romance. In this beginning section, the poet omitted Tristram's killing of Morhault, Irish Yseult's uncle, an act that gains the knight fame by allowing him to save Cornwall from monetary taxation and tributes of human lives. Further, Swinburne does not have Tristram arrive in Cornwall glorifying Yseult, so that his uncle will want her for his bride. Mark somehow already knows of and desires Yseult when Tristram arrives.

This focus upon style rather than content continues throughout the poem, and is especially evident in canto 2, which begins with a discussion of Yseult's almost unworldly beauty. Tristram is instantly captivated (before the love potion is consumed) and, like a typical courtly lover, is prepared to die for her even though he feels unworthy of this sacrifice:

> And he would have died in place
> But for love and knightly grace
> That he saw that maiden face.
>
> And he knelt with heart-aflame,
> Took her robe in sight of them,
> Kissed the skirt and kissed the hem.
>
> Ah, dear saints, how well it were,
> Thought he, to die knightly there
> For that lady's golden hair.
>
> And he thought it very good
> He should perish where she stood
> Crowned upon with maidenhood.

> And his whole heart for her sake
> With a large delight did ache
> Till it seemed to burn and break.
>
> And he thought it well and meet,
> Lain before that lady sweet,
> To be trodden by her feet.
>   (II 52-69)

The last stanza of this passage is an example of Swinburne's "erotic and sadomasochistic" interest (A. Harrison 79). This coupling of love and physical pain is more intense in the third canto, which opens after Tristram and Yseult have consumed the magical wine and Yseult has wedded Mark.

In canto 3, following the elaborate nuptial festivities, Tristram sings Yseult's praises "in the sweet French tongue" (III 27). She loves Tristram for his song, just as the second Yseult does, and just as in canto 1 Tristram and the sailors loved the Irish Yseult for her song.[4] After three years of singing and loving, the couple's rendezvous are revealed to King Mark. First, however, Swinburne relates the couple's most difficult and bloody liaison, in which Yseult carries Tristram upon her back to avoid two sets of footprints showing in the snowy path leading to her chamber:

> Then she raised him tenderly,
> Bore him lightly as might be,
> That was wonderful to see.
>
> So they passed by trail and track,
> Slowly, in the night all black,
> And she bore him on her back.
>
> As they twain went along,
> Such great love had made her strong,
> All her heart was full of song.
>
>   . . .
>
> She was hurt with snow and stone,
> Came no sob nor any moan

That with bare feet had she gone.
(III 100-08, 118-20)

Yseult's wounds on her feet and her neck inspire "fierce and bitter kisses" (III 138) from Tristram, and the pain catapults their lovemaking that evening to new heights. The reversal of sexual roles, with Yseult able to tolerate enormous pain and her knight playing a peculiarly inactive role, may indicate that at this time, Swinburne was "unconsciously seeing Tristram as small and passive like him" (Henderson, *Swinburne* 31). (In *Tristram of Lyonesse,* the character is restored to his historic heroic status.)

When Mark, "the king so lean and cold" (III 153), is informed of the adulterous relationship between Tristram and Yseult, he does not force his wife to prove her innocence by carrying hot irons. Swinburne deviates from his sources in handling this situation, simply allowing Yseult to scornfully swear that no man has touched her, unless it was the ill-clad man standing nearby (Tristram in disguise). Mark is temporarily pacified by Yseult's oath, but the Queen nevertheless asks Tristram to leave Cornwall.

Tristram passively accepts Yseult's order by immediately departing for Camelot. Canto 4 concerns his visit to Arthur's court and his subsequent trip to Brittany. Guinevere's beauty reminds Tristram so much of Yseult's glorious looks that the good knight is plagued by memories of "the bitter love" (IV 53) and wishes to escape these painful remembrances. In this canto, the typically compressed technique of the ballad style Swinburne was imitating is especially evident. No explanation is given of Tristram's destination; the knight simply lands in Brittany, a land ruled by the orphaned Queen who, coincidentally, shares Tristram's lover's name. This "Yseult of the white snow-hand" (IV 59) is reminiscent of Arnold's character of the same name because she is described as patient, sweet, and shy.

"For the love of her sweet name" (IV 95), Tristram remains near Yseult of Brittany, though he thinks of her as only a sweet child. Overhearing Tristram singing a song about the "praise that Yseult won" (IV 130), Yseult of Brittany understandably thinks that Tristram returns her love. Without further explanation of

Tristram's lack of devotion to his former lover, we are told of wedding plans:

> And he wist that it were well
> In her quiet love to dwell;
> So their marriage-time befell.
>
> (IV 169-71)

Soon after the couple is betrothed, Tristram thirsts for adventure and sets off for Camelot, where he is once again reminded of the first Yseult by Guinevere's similar beauty. Again, rather than journey in disguise to Cornwall, as he does in the medieval romance, Tristram returns to Brittany.

Canto 5 concentrates upon Tristram's dilemma on his wedding night. In Thomas of Erceldoune's *Sir Tristrem,* the hero feels guilt, increased when the ring of Yseult of Cornwall slips from his finger on the wedding night, symbolizing his betrayal of his first love:

> Tristrem biheld that ring,
> Tho was his hert ful wo;
> "Oyain me swiche a thing,
> Dede never Ysonde so;
> Marke her lord the king,
> With tresoun may hir to;
> Mine hert may no man bring,
> For no thing hir fro,
> That fre;
> Ich have tvinned ous to,
> The wrong is al in me."
>
> (*Sir Tristrem*, fitte 3, stanza 36)

Swinburne's Tristram desires the beautiful, naked wife in his bed, but in his debate about consummation he considers the roles of both women. Yseult of Cornwall's face appears before him, reminding him of his great love for her, but Tristram is equally concerned about dishonoring Yseult of Brittany:

> And great shame will overtake
> All her beauty for my sake

If her maidenhood I break.

And this thing shall never be
That for maiden love of me
Men should shame her as they see.

For some men will say, "Behold,
Yseult queen, the hair of gold
Was his paramour of old."

(V 52-60)

Tristram prays that Christ will grant him the strength to refrain from deflowering his wife, and the canto ends with Yseult "sleeping in her maidenhood" (V 141).

The loneliness of Yseult of Cornwall and her fears that Tristram is dead are the focus of canto 6. Her torment parallels Tristram's, but her sorrow is greater; not only must Yseult mourn the loss of her lover, but she also is faced with Mark's growing envy and hatred.[5] Swinburne has consistently blackened the character of Mark until, in this last canto, the King appears as a cruel and vindictive drunkard. The poem ends abruptly with Yseult gloomily considering her diminishing beauty and Mark's hatred for her.

Swinburne's treatment of his subject in 1857 contains a hint of themes to be developed later in *Tristram of Lyonesse*, the poet's more mature approach to the Tristram and Iseult story. The early work contains many of the same social, psychological, and emotional entanglements, but they are not amplified by the long philosophic passages so prevalent in the later poem. Also, the ballad like diction, simple and frequently monosyllabic, contributes to "Queen Yseult"'s atmosphere of childlike simplicity and often masks complex situations. Perhaps not yet capable of producing the ideological and ecstatic lyrical passages that dominate *Tristram of Lyonesse*, the young Swinburne first related the story with little artistic embellishment.

Swinburne's other early Arthurian works are much shorter than "Queen Yseult." "King Ban," published posthumously in 1915, is a melancholic, introspective 120-line fragment based loosely on the *Morte*. Unlike Malory's equivalent scene, however,

Ban is not saved by King Arthur. Besieged by the forces of
Claudas and betrayed by his own seneschal, Swinburne's Ban
surveys the destruction of his kingdom and prays, like Christ, that
he will not be forsaken. Ban waits in vain for Arthur to aid him:

> Because that time King Arthur would not ride,
> But lay and let his hands weaken to white
> Among the stray gold of a lady's head.
> His hands unwedded: neither could bring help
> To Ban that helped to rend his land for him
> From a steel wrist of spoilers, but the time
> A sleep like yellow mould had overgrown,
> A pleasure of sweet and sick as marsh-flowers.
>   (28-35)

In the early chapters of the *Morte*, Ban is protected by the heroic
young Arthur. However, in Swinburne's poem, Ban's personal
reflections in his final soliloquy reflect a spirit crushed by the stark
realization that he has been abandoned: [6]

> Therefore I pray you, O God marvellous,
> See me how I am stricken among men,
> And how the lip I fed with plenteousness
> And cooled with wine of liberal courtesy
> Turns a snake's life to poison me and clings--
>   (116-120)

In "King Ban" are the ironic and muted seeds that are developed
later in *Tristram of Lyonesse* and *The Tale of Balen* into a full
blown challenging of the powers of Arthur and the Christian God.

In "The Day before the Trial," an apparently completed
poem of 44 lines, first published by George Lafourcade in 1928,
Swinburne recast the scene of Morris's "The Defence of
Guenevere," and portrayed Arthur's feelings about the accusations
against his wife. Not the proud king of Malory's work, the Arthur
of Swinburne's poem is filled with self-pity and anguish:

> And I grow old waiting here,
> Grow sick with pain of Guenevere,

> My wife, that loves not me.
>
> (4-6)

The entire poem is a melancholy soliloquy in which Arthur discusses not only his suspicions about his wife, but also his "dull hate of Launcelot" (28). Strangely, Arthur calls Launcelot "pure of sin" (30) and "clean as any maid" (31). The King compares himself unfavorably with his knight because, of the two, only Launcelot has been blessed from God:

> But I, a woman's hands there weighed
> Instead of God's upon my head,
> No maid was I, to see
> The white Sangreal borne up in air,
> To touch at last God's body fair,
> To feel strange terror stir my hair
> As a slow light went past.
>
> (34-40)

With the phrase "a woman's hands," Arthur may refer to his incestuous relationship with Morgause, but it seems more likely, given Arthur's description of Launcelot as a "maid," that the King believes that Guenevere has soiled her husband, but has not lain with her favorite knight. These questions remain unanswered, and the poem ends with Arthur lamenting that he must endure the hateful glances of his wife who does not love him.

"And she loves not me" is a concluding line, again concerning Guenevere, spoken by the protagonist of "Lancelot." This poem, a dramatization in which Lancelot is visited by an angel who allows him a brief glimpse of the Grail, is 325 lines long and was first printed for private circulation in 1915. "Lancelot" is similar to "The Day before the Trial" because it is written in the same verse form, and because it continues the story immediately after Guenevere's trial. In "Lancelot," the knight has rescued the Queen before she was to be consumed by fire, and they now live together at Joyeuse Garde.

With Lancelot's visitation by an angel and the emphasis on the Grail Quest, the poem is similar to Morris's "Sir Galahad, a Christmas Mystery." Lancelot's failure on the quest, caused by his sinful love of Guenevere, contrasts with his son Galahad's more successful adventures. "Lancelot" is also similar to Morris's "King Arthur's Tomb"; in both poems the atmosphere is hot and oppressive, the Queen rejects Lancelot because she feels that the kingdom has been destroyed by their love, and Guenevere's ordeal has caused her once great beauty to fade.

Perhaps the primary source for Swinburne's "Lancelot" was visual, stemming from Rossetti's Oxford Union mural *Launcelot at the Shrine of the Sanc Grael* (Cochran *Arthuriana* 58). Rossetti explained his painting in a July 1858 letter to Charles Eliot Norton:

> Sir Lancelot is prevented by his sin from entering the chapel of the Sanc Grael. He has fallen asleep before the shrine full of angels. And between him and it, rises in his dream the image of Queen Guenevere, the cause of all. She stands gazing at him with her arms extended in the branches of an apple tree. (*Family Letters* 1: 242-43)

Rossetti's description of this painting is echoed by Swinburne's plot. The poem opens in autumn after Lancelot has searched in vain all summer for the Grail. Exhausted by his long ride, the knight stops by a chapel and drifts into a somnolent state. After recalling his futile summer of searching, Lancelot is visited by an angel, who allows him a partial viewing of the Grail, which is soon obstructed by a shadowy picture of Guenevere, standing under a tree. This vision of the woman who prevented Lancelot's success in his adventure provokes a prolonged and bitter self-examination by the knight. Ultimately, Lancelot seems more disappointed that Guenevere will not consent to be his Queen than he is that he is unable fully to view the Grail:

> Vain was the prayer I prayed alway,
> Where in evil case I lay,
> That she might love me one day
> And the manner is;
> Vain the prayer that I have prayed,
> That, lying between light and shade,
> I that loved her as I said,

> I that never kissed a maid,
> I might have her kiss.

(318-26)

As in a poem of the medieval dream-vision genre, this work's protagonist, in his altered state, is able accurately to understand the significance of his life. Lancelot contrasts the two most important features of his life, his love for the Queen and the Grail Quest, and realizes that he will never be able to experience a full triumph in either area. Like Morris's Sir Galahad, Lancelot dramatizes in his sleep trance the struggle between earthly and spiritual love.

In the *Morte*, Launcelot sees the Grail as it heals a sick man. The vision leaves Launcelot unconscious, and upon his recovery, he is asked by a heavenly voice to leave that holy place. The knight realizes that his relationship with Gwenyvere has prevented him from responding more fully to the holy vessel: "And now I take uppon me the adventures to seke of holy thynges, now I se and undirstonde that myne olde synne hyndryth me and shamyth me, that I had no power to stirre nother speke whan the holy bloode appered before me" (896; bk. 13, chap. 19). Launcelot's newfound understanding causes him to repent to a holy man "how he had loved a quene unmesurabely and oute of mesure longe" (896; bk. 13, chap. 20), and to perform acts of penance. Later in the narrative, Launcelot attempts to enter a chamber in the Castle Carbenic wherein the Grail shines. Because he has sinned for twenty-four years, his encounter with the Grail leaves him unconscious for twenty-four days. When Launcelot awakens, he does not think of Gwenyvere, but is pleased that God has allowed him the vision: "Why have yee awaked me? For I was more at ease than I am now. A, Jesu Cryste, who myght be so blyssed that myght see opynly Thy grete mervayles of secretnesse there where no synner may be?" (1017; bk. 17, chap. 16). Obviously, Swinburne's conception of Lancelot is based less upon Malory's repentant knight than upon Morris's constantly devoted lover. Staines suggests that at this period in Swinburne's life, "Malory was an inspiration as yet seen primarily through the eyes of Morris" ("Swinburne" 58).

Swinburne's last short Arthurian poem, "Joyeuse Garde," was also directly inspired by Morris, in this case another Oxford mural "How Sir Palomydes loved La Belle Iseult with exceeding great love, but how she loved him not but rather Sir Trystram."[7] The poem expands an episode from the *Morte* in which Tristram and Iseult are reunited at Launcelot's castle. Swinburne's focus in this work, the satisfying lovemaking of the couple, is described in the sort of highly erotic terms Malory never attempted. These descriptions of carnal love would certainly have offended Victorian audiences but, like Swinburne's other short Arthurian works, this poem was published posthumously, A 78-line narrative fragment of iambic pentameter, the work was first printed for private circulation in *A Day of Lilies* (1918).

"Joyeuse Garde" may have been intended as a continuation of "Queen Yseult" because the meeting at Lancelot's castle is traditionally the next stage in the Tristram and Iseult narrative. "Queen Yseult" concluded with the lady's reflections about her abandonment by Tristram and her fear of Mark. "Joyeuse Garde" concentrates on the Queen's joyous feelings about her reunion with her lover, but the celebration is marred by her anxiety about Mark's plotting:

> Men say the king
> Hath set keen spies about for many a mile,
> Quick hands to get them gold, sharp eyes to see
> Where your way swerves across them. This long while
> Hath Mark grown older with his hate of me,
> And now his hand for lust to smite at us
> Plucks the white hairs inside his beard that he
> This year made thicker.
>
> (48-55)

This concern about Mark's surveillance is, of course, a great obstacle to the lovers' meetings; yet traditionally the amount of ecstasy experienced by courtly lovers grows in proportion to the degree of danger their trysts generate. In "Joyeuse Garde," Yseult is perfectly able to relax in bed with her knight, despite the threat of Mark's spies:

> Her eyes said "Tristram" now, but her lips held
> The joy too close for any smile or moan

> To move them; she was patiently fulfilled
> With a slow pleasure that slid everwise
> Even into hands and feet, but could not build
> The house of its abiding in her eyes,
> Nor measure any music by her speech.
>   (17-23)

The sensuousness of this description is meager compared to the explicitly erotic encounters the lovers enjoy in Tristram of Lyonesse.

While Swinburne's early Arthurian works have some merits, they are slight when compared to the poet's last two Arthurian poems. Significantly, Swinburne must have been dissatisfied with his youthful efforts, inasmuch as these five poems, with the exception of "Queen Yseult"'s first canto--were all published posthumously; he never consented to widespread publication during his lifetime.

TRISTRAM OF LYONESSE

Whereas Swinburne's early Arthurian poems are marginal to his fame, *Tristram of Lyonesse* can be considered his magnum opus. The poem has been classified as an epic, but it is more lyrical than narrative: "Although Tristram does not adhere strictly to the conventional criteria for narrative and epic poetry by which early critics evaluated it, and in spite of Swinburne's own disclaimers, his highly wrought masterwork is indeed a species of epic, and as such it is an undeniably successful tour de force" (A. Harrison 98-99). Although many early critics, including T. S. Eliot, found the work diffusive, its many non narrative, philosophical passages do build to reflect one coherent ideology. As Kerry McSweeney asserts in "The Structure of Swinburne's *Tristram of Lyonesse*" (1968), the work is carefully constructed and full of important parallelism, such as the matching invocations to Love and Fate that open and close the poem.

Parallelism, recurrent motifs, and the recapitulation of rhymes lend the poem a greatness beyond earlier versions, but do not erode "the frustration produced by the ostensible inaptness of

Swinburne's lyrical approach to a narrative subject" (Reed 99). Swinburne's readers should approach *Tristram of Lyonesse* with a knowledge of major versions of the narrative. Confusing flashbacks, often in beginning midsentence, offer some exposition, but the disjunction they impose, particularly when added to long philosophical passages, makes a casual reading of this poem impossible.

For Victorian reviewers, Swinburne's unorthodox religious values, as exposed in this poem, were somewhat overshadowed by the work's blatant eroticism; the *Saturday Review* labeled the poem "effusively erotic," and the *Spectator* complained that Swinburne painted "the sensual appetite with a redundancy and excess that excite disgust" (Hyder xi). Although the faithfulness of the lovers to each other seems eminently Victorian (Miyoshi 9), Swinburne clearly intended to shock his audience: "By the grace of the Devil, I hope to make the copulation passages of the poem more warm and provocative of sinful appetite than anything my chaste muse has yet attempted" (*Swinburne's Letters* II 90). Modern audiences are more apt to be fascinated by Swinburne's addition of his own views concerning the meaning of human life to the ancient myth than they are likely to be horrified by the overt sexuality.

The fatal passion of the medieval romance becomes, in Swinburne's poem, a celebration of human passion and sexual love. Because the poem shows Iseult learning to cherish Tristram's pantheistic philosophy, the work also seeks to erode the rock of Christianity. From its opening lines to its conclusion, *Tristram of Lyonesse* is about four lips that "become one burning mouth" (I 136). Although this love is doomed and bleak, the lovers reach fulfillment with each other and with the universe of nature that surrounds and encourages them: "Perhaps it is *because* the lovers are so clearly foredoomed that Swinburne could write so richly of their fulfillment. In this central legend symbolizing the love-sickness of the western world, Swinburne creates by far his healthiest love poetry" (Rosenberg, "Swinburne" 136). Tristram and Iseult are motivated by more than mere carnality; their sexuality merges with a transcendent spirituality that includes all of external nature.

The poet began the work *in medias res*, just before the lovers drink the magical wine. He ignored the early aspects of

Tristram's life to concentrate on the development of the love story, as well as the joy and suffering it engenders. Although love brings pain to Tristram and Iseult, they, like all other men and women, are not free and can live fully only by accepting the experiences of desire. Whereas Tennyson's *Idylls* proposed personal restraint in favor of knightly responsibility, Swinburne glorifies a more hedonistic position; in *Tristram of Lyonesse*, the lovers enjoy greater nobility and a more dignified end precisely because they completely indulge their desires. Swinburne chose to recreate the legend because he felt that it had been degraded by other writers of his era:

> I am working just as hard as I have ever worked towards the completion of a poem in nine parts on the story of Tristram, which is and was in my eyes always the loveliest of mediaeval legends. I do not forget that two eminent contemporaries have been before me in the field, but Arnold has transformed and recast the old legend, and Tennyson--as usual, if I may be permitted to say so--has degraded and debased it. (*Swinburne's Letters* IV: 260)

Expressing in narrative form the metaphysics of love, Swinburne's poem employs the legend as an archetypal illustration of the human condition of perpetual passion. This condition, of course, suffers from mutability, but heroic men and women must accept transition by regarding it as part of a constantly changing yet changeless natural world.

Swinburne retained the inevitable, fated conclusion of the old legend, but the tragedy is redeemed "by sublime participation in a cosmic and self-fulfilling generative force organically governing history, the interactions of men and women, and the relations between men and nature" (A. Harrison 82). None of Swinburne's many possible sources relates the legend in this manner. The poet reacted against Tennyson and Arnold, utilized Wagner and the German Romantics, partially employed Scott's edition of Thomas's *Sir Tristrem* for plot structure, and borrowed heavily from Malory for details. Yet however much the outcome reflects debts to other sources, both medieval and modern,

Tristram of Lyonesse is ultimately Swinburne's private mythology. The poet obviously read most of the Arthurian material available to him. However, the sheer abundance of the possible sources, coupled with the realization that Swinburne used the legend to express completely different views from his predecessors, makes of limited value[8] a search for indebtedness.

In 1871, Swinburne published "Tristram and Iseult, Prelude to an Unpublished Poem." This "Prelude," a lyrical rhapsody on Love's power, announces all the major themes of the fully developed poem, which was not published until 1882. The opening lines of the "Prelude" suggest, through their use of paradox and oxymoronic phrases, Love's power as the force behind the action:

> Love, that is first and last of all things made,
> The light that has the living world for shade,
> The spirit that for temporal veil has on
> The souls of all men woven in unison,
> One fiery raiment with all lives inwrought
> And lights of sunny and starry deed and thought,
> And alway through new act and passion new
> Shines the divine same body and beauty through,
> The body spiritual of fire and light
> That is to worldly noon as noon to night;
> Love, that is flesh upon the spirit of man
> And spirit within the flesh whence breath began;
> Love, that keeps all of the choir of lives in chime;
> Love, that is blood within the veins of time.
>   ("Prelude," Gosse and Wise 1-14)

Through a catalogue of constellations in which each monthly astrological sign represents a heroic and doomed love heroine such as Dido, Helen, or Francesca, Love becomes linked with a natural cyclicity and interdependency that serves to guide the lives of all men. Iseult is part of April, and this is the "Prelude"'s only link to the narrative portion of *Tristram of Lyonesse*. Like the story of Tristram and Iseult, and like all of human existence, the constellations change forever, but remain the same. Swinburne, like Carlyle, was convinced that supreme spiritual truths repeat themselves historically "in individual lives which are governed by a unitary and presiding impulse in the world" (A. Harrison 113). "The sun-god which is love" ("Prelude" 148) shapes the world and is associated with Fate, the ambassador of Love. Those who deny these forces never experience true life:

> Yea, even the shadows of them spiritless,
> Through the dim door of sleep that seem to press,
> Forms without form, a piteous people and blind,
> Men and no men, whose lamentable kind
> The shadow of death and shadow of life compel
> Through semblances, of heaven and false-faced hell,
> Through dreams of light and dreams of darkness tost
> On waves innavigable, are these so lost?
> ("Prelude" 161-68)

We will all one day pass from this world, so, as the "Prelude" suggests, we should live on earth to our fullest potential. The sun-god, Love, is fed by the fame of tragic lovers who accepted their fate, and this deity's radiance is increased by those, like Swinburne, who gave a portion of their days to celebrate these heroic individuals. The jealous orthodox God may seem to doom these lovers unjustly, but he is shown to have no real power; he is unable to deprive any individual of the sleep that naturally follows an exemplary life, so each triumphant human being will eventually pass into a similar state of limbo. Therefore, according to Swinburne, it is best for one to accept completely his destiny so that he may be remembered as an example to future generations. The many ideas incorporated into the "Prelude" are more comprehensible in *Tristram of Lyonesse*, inasmuch as each separate episode in the poem is an example of a portion of Swinburne's rather difficult and involved philosophy. Tristram and Iseult function in the poem as models of lovers who survive the torments and navigate around the obstacles of the world to reach full consummation of love through a death that allows them fulfillment. The man-made concepts of God and time are Love's chief enemies, but they are powerless.

Tristram of Lyonesse, Swinburne's unique synthesis of passion, pantheism, and courtly love, appeared in its complete form of a prelude and nine cantos in 1882. Canto I, "The Sailing of the Swallow," begins with a description of the young, beautiful, and innocent Tristram and Iseult before they drink the wine. Iseult questions Tristram about the inhabitants of Camelot, and the knight's answers provide a background for the legend, as well as the framework for Swinburne's iconoclastic vision.[9] Arthur's "sightless sin unknown" (I 530) with his sister Morgause may be unforgivable by a wrathful God, but Tristram knows that men will remember the king for his greatness rather than for this one innocent and unfortunate act. Iseult does not understand why God should be less forgiving than his creatures on earth: "Great pity it is and strange it seems to me / God could not do them so much right as we, / Who slay not men for witless evil done" (I 598-600). Thus begins the conflict of the two religious systems that are constantly opposed in the poem: orthodox Christianity versus the power of Fate and Love.

The fatal passion of Merlin for Nimue is Tristram and Iseult's next topic of conversation and becomes in the rest of the poem, beyond simply another example of a predestined relationship, a recurrent vision of the perfect example of love. Merlin is allowed a permanent and delightful state of sleep amid woodland elements, when he is touched by "the heavenly hands of holier Nimue" (I 709). This exalted position for Nimue is Swinburne's invention and is an appropriate change, befitting his vision of true lovers able to experience an organic unity with the earth.

Through the denizens of Camelot, Tristram teaches Iseult about love, and then he underscores this education with two songs. His lessons are so successful that Iseult suddenly feels a desire to experience this emotion herself. Previously described as an undeveloped flower, Iseult now blossoms under the radiant influence of the sun god and Tristram:

> And Iseult mused and spake no word, but sought
> Through all the hushed ways of her tongueless thought
> What face or covered likeness of a face
> In what veiled hour or dream-determined place
> She seeing might take for love's face, and believe
> This was the spirit to whom all spirits cleave.
> For that sweet wonder of the twain made one

> And each one twain, incorporate sun with sun,
> Star with star molten, soul with soul imbued,
> And all the soul's works, all their multitude,
> Made one thought and one vision and one song,
> Love--this thing, this, laid hand on her so strong
> She could not choose but yearn till she should see.
> (I 850-62)

With Iseult's desire developed, the potion now seals their fate.[10] While still aboard the *Swallow* the lovers indulge their yearning and are deliriously happy until they land in Cornwall.

Canto 2, "The Queen's Pleasance," introduces King Mark, "a swart lean man" with "cold unquiet eyes," who is "close-mouthed, gaunt-cheeked, wan as a morning moon" (II 64-66). Iseult marries Mark, but substitutes her attendant Brangwain in the bridal bed.[11] When Iseult slips between the sheets, replacing Brangwain at the light of dawn, Mark's musings concerning the wonder of his having lain with this ethereal woman are ironic. Iseult experiences carnal love with no man but the radiant sun-worshipper, Tristram. Palamede, who kidnaps the Queen soon after the wedding, is also unable to touch Iseult, "for awe / Constrained him, and the might of love's high law" (II 214-15).

Tristram rescues Iseult from the overawed knight and takes her deep into the woods, where they remain undisturbed for some time.[12] The lovers experience a spiritual and physical fusion with each other, as well as a transcendental harmony with nature. Iseult, having learned well Tristram's philosophy, is the first to realize that this perfect time cannot last. She understands that the best solution to their dilemma is immediate death:

> Only with stress of soft fierce hands she prest
> Between the throbbing blossoms of her breast
> His ardent face, and through his hair her breath
> Went quivering as when life is hard on death;
> And with strong trembling fingers she strained fast
> His head into her bosom; till at last
> Satiate with sweetness of that burning bed,
> His eyes afire with tears, he raised his head

> And laughed into her lips; and all his heart
> Filled hers; then face from face fell, and apart
> Each hung on each with panting lips, and felt
> Sense into sense and spirit in spirit melt.
> "Hast thou no sword? I would not live till day,
> O love, this night and we must pass away,
> It must die soon, and let us not die late."
>   (II 379-93)

Indeed, in the next canto, "Tristram in Brittany," change arrives to part the lovers. Although the last canto concluded with the pair in their forest bower, this canto opens with Tristram lamenting that he has been divided from Iseult for three years. Tristram views this separation in terms of death:

> We have loved and slain each other, and love yet.
> Slain; for we live not surely, being in twain:
> In her I lived, and in me she is slain,
> Who loved me that I brought her to her doom,
> Who loved her that her love might be my tomb.
>   (III, 8-12)

The lovers have been divided by Mark's discovery of their relationship. Not wishing to make the decisions of the love-sun-fate god look foolish, Tristram vows not to ask that his bitter fate be reversed:

> And though ye had mercy, I think I would not pray
> That ye should change your counsel or your way
> To make our life less bitter.
>
>   . . .
>
> What man would stretch forth hand on them to make
> Fate mutable, God foolish, for his sake?
>   (V 123-25, 129-30)

In the end, Tristram's lack of resistance proves the most practical course because Fate is a benevolent deity who does not enforce punishment for joy and who allows a sleeping death, the only release from courtly love.

After Tristram suffers banishment from Cornwall, his lonely wanderings bring him into contact with Iseult of Brittany, a sweet young maiden who becomes the final insurmountable obstacle to the lovers' fufillment on earth. After a brief courtship, Tristram and Iseult of Brittany are married. Not wishing to violate completely his vow to his former lover, Tristram denies his desire for his wife. The knight is persuaded to leave Iseult of Brittany in her virginal state when he recalls the greater beauty of Iseult of Cornwall. Canto 5, "Iseult at Tintagel," relates the Irish Iseult's thoughts on this same evening as she and the hound Hodain (who licked a bit of the magical wine) pine for Tristram. Fearing that the vindictive Christian God will punish Tristram with eternal damnation for his trysts with her, Mark's wife attempts to renounce her love for the knight. She prays that Tristram will forget her so that she will not see him in hell. Iseult refuses to repent of her adultery, knowing that the fires of hell will never be able to consume her great love.

Then it is the turn of Iseult to rebuke the orthodox God for his lack of pity:

> Hath thou no care, that all we suffer yet?
> What help is ours of thee if thou forget?
> What profit have we though thy blood were given,
> If we that sin bleed and be not forgiven?
> Not love but hate, thou bitter God and strange,
> Whose heart as man's heart hath grown cold with change,
> Not love but hate thou showest us that have sinned.
>   (V 263-69)

To pacify this vengeful God, Iseult offers, as the price for Tristram's salvation, to accept all the punishment for their sin upon herself.

Iseult's feelings of desperation are dissolved not by mercy from God, but by a final meeting with her lover in the next canto, "Joyous Garde." Tristram's philosophical counsel encourages in Iseult a recognition of the didactic power of nature, and she is finally able to resign herself to fate. The fear of divine retribution dissolves when Iseult realizes that love leads one through death to peace. The poet of the impossibility of love's survival on earth, Swinburne consistantly associated love with death: "He is of course best known for a variety of that theme--the pain implicit in all pleasure. Virtually incapable of using the word pleasure without its alliterative opposite, Swinburne is undeniably sado-masochistic, but this lurid aspect of his lyricism has obscured his true achievement" (Rosenberg "Swinburne" 137)

In canto 7, "The Wife's Vigil," the omnipotent, transcendent force of Love faces a worthy opponent in its opposite, the God of Christianity. Iseult of Brittany, stung to fury by Tristram's abandonment, makes a hateful supplication to the Old Testament deity, who thrives on fear and hate. The wife prays that she will be allowed to know that the lovers suffer in hell. She does not realize that Tristram and Iseult of Cornwall have made a pact to face death bravely or that her curse is of no consequence because the lovers do not fear divine retribution. All of the wife's former sweetness has been changed to bitterness through her encounter with Tristram. She demands that God render judgment upon her faithless husband and allow her to make Tristram aware, in his last hour, of her feelings about his crime.

The next canto, "The Last Pilgrimage," reinforces the idea that Tristram has no need to fear his wife's deity. The knight is revitalized when he swims in the sea and experiences communion with his true god, Love. The hero is reborn in this mystical fusion with the natural world, ready to face his final battle without fear. He does not have foreknowledge of his fate, but is prepared to accept his destiny. When Tristram receives a mortal wound, he and his wife are both pleased.

The evocation of Fate in the poem's final canto, "The Sailing of the Swan," echoes the "Prelude"'s glorification of Love:

> Fate, that was born ere spirit and flesh were made,
> The fire that fills man's life with light and shade;
>
> . . .
>
> Fate, that of all things save the soul of man
> Is lord and God since body and soul began;
> Fate that keeps all tune of things in chime.
>
> (IX 1-2, 11-13)

   While the poet claims that Fate, the emissary of Love, will overthrow the "miscreant" (IX 90) Christian God, "the head of fear, the false high priest" (IX 86), the reader is concerned for Tristram's safety and salvation. The knight lies dying under the bitter eyes of the white-handed Iseult:

> For only in hope of evil was her life.
> So bitter burned within the unchilded wife
> A virgin lust for vengeance, and such hate
> Wrought in her now the fervent work of fate.
>   (IX 179-82)

Indeed, Iseult of Brittany kills her husband with a word when she lies about the color of the boat's sail, and it seems that victory belongs to the wife and her vengeful God.

   Iseult of Cornwall arrives too late, so a reunion on earth for the lovers is obstructed. However, the angry wife cannot prevent the couple's peaceful union after death. King Mark, having forgiven the lovers, builds a tomb to house their bodies; Swinburne deviates from his sources here when he allows the sea, an important image of eternity, to claim Tristram and Iseult forever. The waves erode the rock upon which Mark has built the chapel, allowing the lovers to be taken into the water, where they will share eternity with the transcendent forces of nature.[13] The final lines of *Tristram of Lyonesse*, indicating the lovers' harmony after difficult lives, prove that Love is the prime mover of the universe, while the God of Christianity is a creation of man's fearful imagination:

> The stroke of love's own hand felt last and best
> Gave them deliverance to perpetual rest.
> So, crownless of the wreaths that life had wound,
> They slept, with flower of tenderer comfort crowned;
>
>   . . .
>
> But peace they have that none may gain who live:
> And rest about them that no love can give,
> And over them, while death and life shall be,

The light and sound and darkness of the sea.

>   (IX 493-96, 573-76)

Swinburne's message appears to be that those who submit to love
as the supreme force in the universe will gain immortality, both
through a peaceful union with spiritual, elemental nature and
through the resurrection of their story by future generations.

THE TALE OF BALEN

In 1895, thirteen years after the publication of *Tristram of
Lyonesse,* Swinburne began composing *The Tale of Balen* (1896).
The poet again argues against a society dominated by the miseries
produced by Christian doctrine:

> He [Swinburne] evokes the knight's [Balen's] English
> history, then, reminds his countrymen of their original
> virtues of courage, honor, and brotherhood and warns them
> back from their long flirtation with Christian ideas.
> Swinburne's loathing for Christianity mellowed somewhat
> in his middle years but returned during the latter part of his
> life, perhaps with greater virulence than ever. . . .
> Christendom is presented in the poem as if it were a
> temporary interruption of a previously established pattern
> of life and character proper to the Englishman but, in
> Arthur's day, preserved only in atavistic heroes like Balen
> who are still nourished from more primitive roots.
> (McGann 266-68)

As the hero of Swinburne's final Arthurian work, Balen is the
perfect representative to complete the poet's discussion of Love
and Fate. Love in *The Tale of Balen*, befitting its feudal context, is
rarely erotic, but rather fraternal or filial, with Balen's dedication
to his fellow men always causing tragedy. Arthur's kingdom is
shown to be infested with evil, even in its early days.

Swinburne's most unoriginal Arthurian poem, *The Tale of
Balen* is almost a paraphrase of the *Morte*'s discussion of this
knight in Book Two, except that the poet makes Malory's plot

seem less haphazardly episodic through the addition of passages intended to increase a reader's understanding of the role of Fate in this knight's life:

> A comparison of Swinburne's poem and its source reveals that the poet wrote his work with an edition of Malory in his hand . . . . The only details Swinburne omitted were the references to the future that are found throughout Malory; since he was not writing his poem as a section of larger work, he included the story within an Arthurian framework without including the references to Galahad and his quest for the Grail, Lancelot and his sin, and the future destruction of the Round Table. (Staines, "Swinburne's" 165-68)

Swinburne's verbal fidelity to the *Morte* is also very noticeable in his descriptive passages. The poem is divided into seven sections of nine-line iambic tetrameter stanzas. The short, balladic lines employ mostly monosyllabic words and frequent repetition.

Despite his nearly exact retelling of Malory's tale, Swinburne personalizes the narrative and adds passages that elevate Balen's tragic stature. This poem's greatness "helps to refute the gradually dissolving commonplace among Victorianists that Swinburne entered his dotage after 1879" (A. Harrison 135). Working to overturn the Victorian idealization of the "Golden Age" of Arthur, Swinburne emphasized Balen's agony, disappointment, and frustration in the world of Camelot. Because Balen was born in Northumbria (like Swinburne), he was able to provide a fresh perspective concerning courtly life. Swinburne's knight is a good, well-meaning man, completely unlike the wild and savage creature of Tennyson's "Balin and Balan." Tennyson's re-creation of the story, with limited fidelity to medieval sources, prompted Swinburne's retelling. Swinburne was, of course, also attracted to Balen as a fatal character of great dignity able to represent a specifically Greek conception of the tragic human condition:[14]

> And I think it has not been found unfit to give something of dignity as well as facility to a narrative which recasts in

modern English verse one of the noblest and loveliest old
English legends. There is no episode in the cycle of
Arthurian romance more genuinely Homeric in its sublime
simplicity and its pathetic sublimity of submission to the
masterdom of fate than that which I have reproduced rather
than recast in "The Tale of Balen." (Swinburne, *Swinburne
Replies* 105)

Whereas Malory's Balan is a victim of his own rashness,
Swinburne inserted unobtrusive references to fate and reinforced
aspects of Balen's innocent hubris to create a more tragic
character. Swinburne's more deterministic version of the tale does
not destroy its medieval spirit, but it does allow the poet to achieve
the "tragic sublimity" at which he aimed.

Tightening the amorphous structure of the tale without
altering Malory's perspective, Swinburne divided the story into
separate parts and paralleled his hero's experiences with the
rhythm of seasonal cycles. Like Tennyson's *Idylls*, Swinburne's
poem concludes with its greatest of many tragedies taking place in
winter. However, Swinburne uses the seasons in another way as
well--to suggest, as he did in *Tristram of Lyonesse*, the idea that
nature and human life are a series of constant repetitions.
Mutability is good and moves the hero toward his fulfillment in
death, the complementary opposite of death.

The poem opens in spring, a season of gaiety and
abandonment that mirrors Balen's youthful search for fame.
Malory's tale begins in Arthur's court, but Swinburne allows the
reader to enjoy the engaging Balen, "a northern child of earth and
sea" (I 14), before he is scarred by the corrupted world of Camelot.
However, even in his early happy days, Balen has a suspicion of
his tragic destiny:

> But alway through the bounteous bloom
> The earth gives thanks if heaven illume
> His soul forefelt a shadow of doom,
> His heart forefelt a gloomier gloom
> Than closes all men's equal ways.
>   (I 28-32)

Immediately upon his arrival at Camelot Balen's unfortunate fate begins when he kills one of King Arthur's despicable relatives and is sent to prison for six months. Malory did not explain the motivation behind the murder; Swinburne's Balen is provoked by insults to his homeland.

In the second part, which begins the four-part summer of Balen's life, the hero proves the wickedness of Arthur's court when he is the only knight pure enough to pull out the maiden's sword, Malison. Balen's refusal to return Malison, even though the maiden tells him that with it he will kill his best friend, reveals his stoic acceptance of fate: "What chance God sends, that chance I take" (II 172). Watching this exchange are other figures who have indulged in impulsive actions. Swinburne omitted Malory's catalogue of the knights who fail in the Malison challenge and replaced it with a list of spectators, who indicate the whole host of problems in Camelot. Morgause, sitting between Guenevere and Iseult, is described in detail. Her glance at Arthur reminds him of their great sin:

> And one in blood and one in sin
> Their hearts caught fire of pain within
> And knew no goal for them to win
> But death that guerdons guilt.
>
> (II 105-08)

In contrast, Balen is full of optimism about his future and departs "with heart of springing hope set free" (II 191).

In part 3, the Lady of the Lake, depicted here as treacherous and cruel, arrives craving a gift from the King as repayment for Excalibur. She demands either the head of Balen or that of the maiden who brought the sword. To avenge the murder of his mother, Balen impetuously decapitates the Lady of the Lake and thus incurs Arthur's wrath. Unable to withstand his monarch's displeasure, Balen sets off to appease Arthur by performing heroic feats. First, however, at the start of the fourth part, Balen must defeat Launceor. Jealous of Balen's success in the sword challenge, Launceor wishes to murder Balen, and his desire is sanctioned by the King. Just as every seemingly innocent act of Balen's has terrible repercussions, his killing of Launceor directly causes another death: Launceor's paramour removes Balen's sword from her lover's body and commits suicide with it.

Balen's sorrow at this point is mitigated by the arrival of his brother Balan. Like Tennyson, and unlike Malory, Swinburne conceived of the brothers as twins. Whereas Tennyson's twins are developed as good and evil--or as two opposite sides of the same person--Swinburne apparently included this change to increase the intensity of fraternal love. Balen experiences "the might of joy in love" (IV 131) when he recognizes his brother, "Twin flower of bright Northumberland, / Twin sea-bird of their loud sea-stand, / Twin song-bird of their morn" (IV 124-26).

Before the brothers ride off in part 5, to capture the renegade King Ryons for King Arthur, Merlin makes one of his many appearances to the knights.[15] The prophet foretells the dolorous blow destined to be struck by Balen because he did not prevent Launceor's lady from killing herself. Balen does not believe that he is capable of such evil and so does not heed Merlin's warning. After the brothers deliver the defeated Ryons to Arthur, they must protect Camelot from Ryons's vengeful supporters. The almost supernatural might of Balan and Balen provokes serious questions from observers: "Strong winds smote the souls of men / If heaven's own host or hell's deep den / Had sent them forth to slay" (V 250-52). Although Balen appears to be a virtuous knight, the destruction he constantly causes seems demonic. His desire for fame and his allegiance to his feudal lord are laudatory, but Balen's courage always proves malevolent.

Part 6 continues Balen's destiny with a new set of adventures that ultimately destroy three entire countries. Arthur dispatches the hero to force a mourning knight to return to the King's forest pavilion. Balen convinces the frightened knight to accept him as his protector and escort to the King, but the knight is killed during the journey by the invisible Garlon. Eventually, after this invisible force has murdered several others, Balen kills Garlon at a festival, and King Pellam, as Garlon's brother, seeks revenge. Losing his weapon, Balen searches Pellam's castle until he discovers a golden spear. In attacking Pellam with this beautiful weapon, Balen strikes the dolorous stroke because this is the spear revered as the one that pierced the side of Christ.

The corrupting of this relic, which was brought to England by Joseph of Arimathea, causes Pellam's castle to collapse and kill everyone inside except for Balen and Pellam. Further, Pellam's deep wound festers for twelve years (until Galahad heals it), and the surrounding lands are destroyed:

> And loud and long from all their folk
> Living, one cry that cursed him broke;
> Three countries had his dolorous stroke
> Slain, or should surely slay.
>
> (VI 555-58)

Balen causes this destruction in the autumn of his life, but the worst is still to come. This knight's personal grief reaches its peak and its release in the winter, beginning in part 7. After he has caused the death of Garnysshe, Duke Hermel's daughter, and an ugly knight, Balen is still pleased with the knowledge that he has undeviatingly followed his fated path. Coming to a castle filled with laughing men and women, Balen is told by the chief lady that he must joust with the knight who guards the island. Most of the female characters in *The Tale of Balen* are treacherous; this lady, whose "face grew bright / as hell-fire" (VII 273-74), is no exception. Before Balen rides out to face the challenger, he is given a new shield so that his brother, the defender of the island, is unable to recognize him. The ladies of the castle joyfully watch as the brothers kill each other.

Balen's dying vision underscores Swinburne's motif of natural cycles as perfect and unchanging. Because he has faced life and death stoically, Balen is granted a paradisiacal vision of his boyhood in Northumberland that "filled his death with joy" (VII 576). As Merlin will later, Balen experiences final harmony with the transcendent forces of nature and expires peacefully:

> So, dying not as a coward that dies
> And dares not look in death's dim eyes
> Straight as the stars on seas and skies
> Whence moon and sun recoil and rise,
> He looked on life and death, and slept.
>
> (VII 577-81)

Like Tristram and Iseult, Balen and Balan gain immortality through acceptance of their inexorable fate. The poem concludes with a reminder that their twin melancholy lives and brave deaths allow them eternal dignity:

This is the tale that memory writes
Of men whose names like stars shall stand,
Balen and Balan, sure of hand,
Two brethren of Northumberland,
In life and death good knights.
(VII 599-603)

With his conception of history as cyclical, Swinburne viewed the Middle Ages as filled with the same agonies to be discovered in any other period. The frustrating moral ambiguities experienced by Balen are never reconciled in the poem because these problems are eternal. The solution suggested, a return to natural primitivism, is clearly impossible in a world dominated by the laws of God and man--rather than those of nature.

CONCLUSION

Even in his early Arthurian works, Swinburne's rebellion against the moral values of his day is evident. When the poet gained independence from Morris's conceptions of the medieval period, he was able to produce two great Arthurian works, *Tristram of Lyonesse* and *The Tale of Balen*, that show their fidelity to the Middle Ages while they simultaneously reflect Swinburne's understanding of the human condition. Deviating from the conceptions of other Victorian writers, Swinburne creates a medieval world in which the characters gain praise if they accept destinies that seem immoral from a Christian perspective.

In Swinburne's relentlessly fatalistic worldview, sorrowful earthly life can be endured only through harmony with nature and personal abandonment to the powers of Love and Fate. The most fortunate of human beings are those who experience the afterlife as a permanent state of somnolence and an organic unity with the earth. These individuals also gain an everlasting and exalted position in the collective memory of mankind.

NOTES

1. The only book-length study of Swinburne's medieval works, *Swinburne's Medievalism: A Study in Victorian Love Poetry* (1988) by Antony H. Harrison, includes a comparison of Swinburne's medievalism with his Hellenism (135-48).

2. In *Swinburne: The Poet in His World* (1979), Donald Thomas harshly describes Swinburne's debt to Morris and the overall effect of the poem: "It's ["Queen Yseult"'s] debt to William Morris was embarrassingly evident, though the embarrassment might have been as much Morris's as Swinburne's. Like a parody, its verses show the worst of the Pre-Raphaelite style and little of the best" (43-44). This reading can be questioned if we view the poem's devices and meanings as a prelude to the epic masterpiece *Tristram of Lyonesse*. Although Swinburne became an expert parodist, and "Queen Yseult" does extend some Pre-Raphaelite devices to their furthest limits, the poet still seems to have been sincere in this early attempt to recast the Tristram and Iseult legend.

3. Gitter's fascinating discussion concerning the literary tradition of golden-haired ladies that "gathered particular force and intensity in the latter half of the nineteenth century" (936), further notes that "the more abundant the hair, the more potent the sexual invitation implied by its display, for folk, literary, and psychoanalytic traditions agree that the luxuriance of the hair is an index of vigorous sexuality, even of wantonness" (938).

4. Harrison makes much of this aesthetic form in his discussion of Queen Yseult finding that "it demonstrates the potential of song to reveal high-truths" (95). While the song lyrics in this poem are not especially philosophical, Swinburne's intellectual depth and ideological concerns are made manifest in the songs included in his more mature work, *Tristram of Lyonesse*.

5. Although Tristram's role in the poem is greater, Swinburne apparently named his work "Queen Yseult" because Yseult's fate is more dismal than Tristram's. Another possible reason for this title is that there are two Queen Yseults in the poem, although Yseult of Cornwall is more frequently discussed.

6. Staines finds that particularly with this final soliloquy, Swinburne's "King Ban" becomes "a study similar to the many portraits of isolated, sad individuals in Morris' first volume of poetry" ("Swinburne's" 57).

7. In "Joyeuse Garde," Swinburne's Tristram refers to the incident depicted in Morris's painting as evidence of his certainty of his lover's fidelity:

> Had I not heart to smile, when Iseult's mouth
> Kissed Palomydes under a thick tree?
> For I remember, as the wind sets low,
> How all that peril ended quietly
> In a green place where heavy sunflowers blow.
>
> (70-74)

8. Staines expressed this reaction as well: "A direct comparison of *Tristram of Lyonesse* and its sources only emphasizes the fact that no comparison is finally valid or helpful to our story" ("Swinburne's" 61).

9. Swinburne's lovers from Camelot are ennobled by various obstructions, a vision faithful to troubadour lyrics; the conventions of courtly love demand a denial of gratification, thereby making death a profound consolation. Tragedies of this nature are exalted and perpetuated by aesthetic works because mankind consistently enjoys the re-creation of sad stories (possibly because "misery loves company"). The Arthurian legends remain enduringly attractive because Camelot was doomed to failure. This material would be of only marginal interest as a story of an ancient and perfect utopia were it unmarred by tragedy.

10. It should be remembered that "although they are innocent before they drain the cup, Swinburne's lovers are predisposed to accept the end that fate has ordained for them" (Cochran "Arthuriana" 71). Tristram and Iseult earlier expressed sympathy for other fated lovers. Further, they are already attracted to each other and are shown as perfectly suited in temperament. The wine simply removes their inhibitions, allowing immediate consummation that might otherwise have been delayed.

11. Swinburne always presents the lovers in their most attractive light, so it is little wonder that he chooses to omit Iseult's subsequent attempt on the life of her maid. The source he follows most closely, *Sir Tristrem* does in the second fitt include this blight on Iseult's character.

12. The love-making scene here is so intense that Theodore Watts-Dunton, the critic and man of letters who took Swinburne into his home in 1879 when the poet was on the brink of an alcoholic collapse, feared that the work would land Swinburne in Central Criminal Court. The poem, published in *Tristram of Lyonesse and Other Poems* (1882) was softened by Swinburne's inclusion of less objectionable poems in the book, particularly those concerning children (Thomas 213).

13. In having the lovers' tomb engulfed by the ocean, Swinburne reminds his audience of the legend that Lyonesse, a region of Cornwall, was eventually swept entirely away by the sea. According to *The Arthurian Encyclopedia*, this legend is not devoid of factual foundation because part of

this area, now Mount's Bay, was above water and inhabited in the early Christian era (Lacy 344). Lyonesse is also usually noted as the site of Arthur's last battle, so Excalibur waits with the Lady of the Lake in this area for the King's return. The Isle of Avalon, resting place of the blessed, is also nearby.

14. As Anthony Harrison points out, the medieval romancers used primarily Trojan and Arthurian themes as sources for subject matter and often revealed a similarity between the two periods (c. f. the first and last stanzas of *Sir Gawain and the Green Knight*). This connection was seldom made in the nineteenth century.

15. Merlin's role of self-appointed messenger between Arthur and Balen is in the *Morte*. However, Swinburne adds to Merlin's function by including passages regarding the wise man's fated eternal union with nature. Thus Merlin serves much the same function in this work as he did in *Tristram of Lyonesse*.

Chapter 6

Final Remarks

Arthurian legends will never be irrelevant because in any historical period the universal themes of guilty love, idealism, and fated doom are pertinent to the human condition. Victorian poets, like their predecessors, often employed these legends as a veneer for social criticism. They did not attempt to reflect accurately historical reality so much as to produce religious, aesthetic, and political systems of representation capable of shaping readers' ideas of how life should be experienced. By reworking already ideological discourses, they hoped through literature to expose societal conflicts and to promote human change. Thus the story of Camelot does not survive as a curio of medieval civilization, but as a vehicle for a broad spectrum of timeless issues. Certainly the exotic atmosphere is particularly entertaining, but Arthurian legends, even in the medieval period, have been consistently used to inspire rather than simply to amuse.

A moral emphasis upon orthodox Christianity is especially evident in Tennyson's *Idylls* a work that condemns the passion of Lancelot and Guinevere. This poetry about Victorian figures in medieval costumes reflects a depressing view of animalistic human beings incapable of redemption or acceptance of their ideal monarchs dutiful code. Tennyson's reworking of Malory is clearly an attempt to discourage wicked conduct among audience members. The *Idylls* is a series of moral lessons about a civilization that steadily progresses toward failure because of the corrosive and contagious nature of human sexuality; sensual creatures are clearly incapable of proper social duty because their emphasis upon self-indulgence creates disloyalty to the common cause. Cynical characters in a blighted world, Tennyson's Arthurian figures are dedicated only to excess. As social criticism, the Arthurian works of Tennyson show that the rigidity required of total commitment to any one cause does not allow for the normal complexity of life. This type of blindness does nothing to further spiritual human love, but produces disastrous deaths.

Arnold, with a more understated approach, echoes Tennyson's concern with moderation; "Tristram and Iseult" reflects less of Christian didacticism and more of a concern about family values. Arnold had little sympathy for the lovers and did not excuse their passion as fated or drug induced. His emphasis upon Iseult of Brittany as an abandoned wife and his invention of her two small children seem intended to reflect the problems immoral love creates in the domestic sphere.

Arnold also used this poem to attack his modern world as a place driven by obsessions that gradually consume spirituality. The solution proposed seems to be a retreat into imagination and calming aesthetic pleasures. If individuals learn to distinguish universal themes in art, Arnold's theory is that their own concerns will be deflected and thereby lessened in importance. As does the hectic pace of life, passion and melancholy cloud understanding of the value of real family love. Further, the loss of creativity destroys spirituality, increasing a sense of confinement on earth and decreasing expectations of the afterlife.

In his colorful depictions of the Arthurian characters, Morris explored personal motivations for many actions that remain unexplained in Malory's *Morte*. Morris's poems reflect a fascination with immoral sexual love in the lives of characters who vacillate between sensual self-indulgence and spiritual puritanism. Guilt promotes a desire for death, but also causes serious anxiety about heavenly salvation. In a nonjudgmental manner, Morris exposes the lack of coalescence between divine love and erotic passion. His powerful, brief depictions of single events from the *Morte* are the most realistic of the Victorian reworkings. In simple language, Morris examined passion as both a creative and destructive force in relation to both God and man.

Ultimately, the poet seemed to realize that earthly and heavenly love are impossible to compare--probably because the faith implicit in Christianity does not allow for factual scrutiny.

Swinburne's Arthurian poems show this same moral concern, but he finds the Christian God to be a figment of fearful human imaginations. As an iconoclastic atheist, the poet rebelled against the limits of Victorian morality by presenting Christianity as revengeful but feeble. Attaching his personal philosophical stance to the old narratives while retaining the structure of his medieval sources, Swinburne glorified human passion. Blatantly erotic at times, his poems praise individuals who do not deviate from predetermined paths. These heroic individuals are encouraged by the tranquil and changeless forces of nature.

In Swinburne's Arthurian works, service to the true gods of Love and Fate allows human beings nobility and dignity. Like the other Victorian poets, Swinburne employs these legends as archetypal examples of the human condition, but he depicts individual human lives guided by a unitary impulse in elemental nature. Supreme spiritual truths are cyclical, like all of the cosmos, so human beings must learn to regard mutability as beneficial because it brings them closer to a peaceful, somnolent state in death. Swinburne shows that those who revere the powerless Christian God and consider that following Fate is immoral are not the type of individuals likely to gain worldly permanence as examples to succeeding generations.

Those Victorian poets who employed Arthurian myth all did so to reflect particular moral stances. The position of Tennyson, the poet laureate, was, of course, least offensive to Victorian audiences. The other views seem to become increasingly rebellious in terms of adherence to Christian values. This sort of reaction, as well as a feeling that the legends are confined within a moral system inapplicable to the time in which Arthur may have existed, has led to twentieth-century interpretations of Arthurian legends that celebrate the period's paganism. In keeping with the habit of re-creating the Camelot narrative to discuss social problems, some recent writers have created feministic Arthurian worlds.

Whether one views the fall of Camelot as caused by the passion between Lancelot and Guinevere or by the incestuous coupling of Arthur and Morgause, the destruction ultimately came about because of illicit love. The dolorous ends of these medieval characters and of a utopian dream in the brutal British past is attributed in every age to the same conflicts of loyalty presented through Malory's fatalistic vision. Chivalry and other nobly conceived ideals cannot survive the failings of human nature. Contemporary and future writers may approach Arthurian legends with new techniques and themes, but they cannot eradicate the final tragedy in which love leads to death.

Selected Bibliography

PRIMARY SOURCES

Arnold, Matthew. *The Works of Matthew Arnold*. 15 vols. London: Macmillan, 1903-04.

Brengle, Richard, ed. *Arthur, King of Britain*. Englewood Cliffs, NJ: Prentice, 1964.

Buckley, Jerome Hamilton and George Benjamin Woods, eds. *Poetry Of the Victorian Period*. 3rd ed. Chicago: Scott, 1965.

Carlyle, Thomas. *Works*. Ed. H. D. Traill. 30 vols. New York: Scribner, 1896-1901.

Froissart, Jean. *The Chronicles of Froissart*. Trans. Lord Berners. Ed. G. C. Macauley. New York: Collier, 1910.

Garbáty, Thomas J., ed. *Medieval English Literature*. Lexington, MA: Heath, 1984.

Layamon. *Brut*. Ed. Sir Frederic Madden. London: Society of Antiquaries, 1847.

Malory, Thomas. *The Works of Sir Thomas Malory*. Ed. Eugène Vinaver. 3 vols. continuously paged. Oxford: Clarendon, 1967.

Morris, William. *The Defence of Guenevere and Other Poems*. Reprint from the Kelmscott Press Edition. London: Longmans, 1900.

Rossetti, Dante Gabriel. *Dante Gabriel Rossetti: His Family Letters*. Ed. William Michael Rossetti. 2 vols. London: Roberts, 1895.

Swinburne, Algernon Charles. *La Jeunesse de Swinburne 1837-67*. Ed. Georges Lafourcade, Paris: Societé d'Edition, 1928.

---. *Poems and Ballads*. Ed. Morse Peckham. New York: Bobbs, 1970.

---. *Swinburne's Letters*. Cecil Y. Lang, ed. New Haven: Lang, 1960.

---. *Swinburne Replies: Notes on Poems and Reviews*. Ed. Clyde Kenneth Hyder. Syracuse: Syracuse University Press, 1966.

---. *Works.* Sir Edmund Gosse and Thomas James Wise, eds. New York: Russell, 1968.

Tennyson, Alfred. *A Collection of Poems by Alfred Tennyson.* Ed. Christopher Ricks. Garden City, NY: Doubleday, 1972.

---. *Idylls of the King.* 1891. New York: Heritage Club, 1939.

---. *Idylls of the King.* Ed. J. M. Gray. London: Penguin, 1983.

Thomas of Erceldoune. *Sir Tristrem.* 1804. Ed. Sir Walter Scott. Edinburgh: Constable, 1819.

SECONDARY SOURCES

Adams, Steven. *The Art of the Pre-Raphaelites.* London: Apple, 1988.

Amor, Anne Clark. *William Holman Hunt: The True Pre-Raphaelite.* London: Constable, 1989.

Angeli, Helen Rossetti. *Pre-Raphaelite Twilight: The Story of Charles Augustus Howell.* London: Richards, 1954.

App, August J. *Lancelot in English Literature.* New York: Haskell, 1965.

Banham, Joanna, and Jennifer Harris, eds. *William Morris and the Middle Ages.* Manchester: Manchester University Press, 1984.

Balch, Dennis R. "Guenevere's Fidelity to Arthur in 'The Defence of Guenevere' and 'King Arthur's Tomb.'" *Victorian Poetry* 13 (1975) 61-70.

Barber, Richard, ed. *The Arthurian Legend.* New York: Dorset, 1985.

Barcus, James E. "(Re)playing and (Re)writing the Quest in Tennyson's 'Gareth and Lynette.'" *The Arthurian Myth of Quest and Magic.* Ed. William E. Tanner. Dallas: Caxton's, 1993. 29-37.

Baum, Paull F. *Ten Studies in the Poetry of Matthew Arnold.* Durham: Duke University Press, 1958.

Berry, Ralph. "A Defense of Guenevere." *Victorian Poetry* 9 (1971): 277-86.

Bloom, Harold, ed. *Pre-Raphaelite Poets.* New York: Chelsea, 1986.

Bonney, William. "Tennyson's Sublunary Grail." *Philological Quarterly* 72.2 (Spring 1993): 237-59.

Bradbrook, M. C. "Malory and the Heroic Tradition." *Arthur, King of Britain.* Ed. Richard L. Brengle. Englewood Cliffs, NJ: Prentice Hall, 1964. 392-95.

Brewer, D. S. "the hoole booke." *Middle English Survey.* Ed. Edward Vasta. Notre Dame, IN: University of Notre Dame Press, 1965. 233-58.

Brooks, Roger L. "Matthew Arnold's Revision of *Tristram and Iseult.*" *Victorian Poetry* 2 (1964): 57-63.

Buckler, William E. *On the Poetry of Matthew Arnold.* New York: New York University Press, 1982.

Burchell, S. C. "Tennyson's 'Allegory in the Distance.'" *PMLA* 68 (1953): 418-24.

Burne-Jones, Edward. *Pre-Raphaelite Drawings by Burne-Jones.* New York: Dover, 1981.

Carley, James P. Introduction. *Matthew Arnold and William Morris*. Wolfeboro, NH: Boydell, 1990, 1-21.

Carsoni, Angela. "Morris' Guenevere: A Further Note." *Philological Quarterly* 42 (1963) 131-34.

Chickering, Howell D., ed. *Beowulf*. Garden City, NY: Doubleday, 1977.

Clark, Kenneth. *The Gothic Revival: An Essay in the History of Taste*. New York: Humanities, 1970.

Cochran, Rebecca. "An Assessment of Swinburne's Arthuriana." *King Arthur Through the Ages*. Ed. Valerie M. Lagorio and Mildred Leake Day. New York: Garland, 1990. 62-80.

---. "Swinburne's Concept of the Hero in 'The Tale of Balen.'" *Arthurian Interpretations* 1 (1986): 47-53.

Connolly, Thomas E. *Swinburne's Theory of Poetry*. New York: State University of New York, 1964.

Cooper, Robyn. "The Relationship between the Pre-Raphaelite Brotherhood and Painters before Raphael in English Criticism of the Late 1840's and 1850's." *Victorian Studies* 24 (1981): 405-438.

Culler, A. Dwight. *Imaginative Reason: The Poetry of Matthew Arnold*. New Haven: Yale University Press, 1966.

Dahl, Curtis. "Morris's 'The Chapel in Lyoness': An Interpretation." *Studies in Philology*. 51 (1954): 482-91.

Daly, Gay. *Pre-Raphaelites in Love*. London: Collins, 1989.

Davis, Mary Byrd. "Matthew Arnold and the Nightmare of History." *Philological Quarterly* 55 (1978): 96-112.

DeLaura, David J. "Matthew Arnold and the Nightmare of History." *Victorian Papers*. London: Edward Arnold, 1972. 41-47.

Dillon, Steven C. "Scandals of War: The Authority of Tennyson's *Idylls*." *Essays in Literature* 18.2 (Fall 1991): 180-95.

Doughty, Oswald. *A Victorian Romantic: Dante Gabriel Rossetti*. 2nd ed. London: Oxford University Press, 1960.

Drinkwater, John. *Swinburne: An Estimate*. 1913. New York: Archon, 1969.

Dunlop, John Colin. *History of Prose Fiction*. 1896. New York: Franklin, 1970.

Eggers, J. Philip. *King Arthur's Laureate*. New York: New York University Press, 1971.

Ellis, Deborah S. "Balin, Mordred, and Malory's Idea of Treachery." *English Studies* 68 (1987): 66-74.

Federman, Raymond, ed. *Surfiction· Fiction Now--and Tomorrow*. 2nd ed. Chicago: Swallow, 1981.

Felluga, Dino Franco. "Tennyson's *Idylls*: Pure Poetry, and the Market." *Studies in English Literature, 1500-1900* 37.4 (Autumn 1997), 783-803.

Fisher, Benjamin Franklin, IV. "Swinburne's *Tristram of Lyoness* in Process." *Texas Studies in Language and Literature* 14 (1972): 509-28.

Fries, Maureen. "What Tennyson Really Did to Malory's Women." *Quondam et Futurus* 1.1 (Spring 1991), 44-55.

Garbáty, Thomas J., ed. *Medieval English Literature*. Lexington, MA: Heath, 1984.

Gaunt, William. *The Pre-Raphaelite Dream*. New York: Schocken, 1966.

Gilbert, Elliot L. "The Female King: Tennyson's Arthurian Apocalypse." *PMLA* 98 (1983): 863-78.

Girouard, Mark. *The Return to Camelot: Chivalry and the English Gentleman.* New Haven: Yale University Press, 1981.

Gitter, Elisabeth G. "The Power of Women's Hair in Victorian Imagination." *PMLA* 99 (1984), 936-54.

Grennan, Margaret R. *William Morris: Medievalist and Revolutionary.* 1945. New York: Russell, 1970.

Gurteen, Stephen Humphreys Villiers. *The Arthurian Epic.* New York: Haskell, 1965.

Hare, Humphrey. *Swinburne: A Biographical Approach.* 1949. New York: Kennikat, 1970.

Harrington, David V. "The Conflicting Passions of Malory's Sir Gawain and Sir Lancelot."*Arthurian Interpretations* Spring 7 (1987): 64-69.

Harrison, Antony H. *Swinburne's Medievalism: A Study in Victorian Love Poetry.* Baton Rouge: Louisiana State University Press, 1988.

Harrison, Martin, and Bill Waters. *Burne-Jones.* 1973. London: Barrie, 1989.

Hellstrom, Ward. *On the Poems of Tennyson.* Gainesville: University Press of Florida, 1972.

Henderson, Philip. *William Morris: His Life, Work and Friends. 1967.* London: André Deutsch, 1986.

---. *Swinburne; Portrait of a Poet.* New York: Macmillan, 1974.

Hilton, Timothy. *The Pre-Raphaelites.* 1970. London: Thomas, 1989.

Hodgson, Amanda. "'The Highest Poetry': Epic Narrative in *The Earthly Paradise* and *Idylls of the King.*" *Victorian Poetry* 34.3 (Autumn 1996): 341-54.

---. *The Romances of William Morris.* Cambridge: Cambridge University Press, 1987.

Hollow, John Walter. "William Morris and the Judgement of God." *PMLA* 86 (1971): 446-51.

Holman, C. Hugh, and William Harmon. *A Handbook to Literature.* 5th ed. New York: Macmillan, 1986.

Hueffer, Ford Madox. *Memories and Impressions: A Study in Atmospheres.* New York: Harper, 1911.

Hughes, Linda K. "All That Makes a Man: Tennyson's *Idylls of the King* as a Primer for a Modern Gentleman." *Arthurian Interpretations* 1 (1986): 54-63.

---. "Tennyson's Urban Arthurians." *King Arthur through the Ages.* Ed. Valerie M. Lagorio and Mildred Leake Day. Vol. II. New York: Garland, 1990. 39-61.

Hunt, John Dixon. *The Pre-Raphaelite Imagination 1848-1900.* Lincoln: University of Nebraska Press,1968.

---. "The Poetry of Distance: Tennyson's 'Idylls of the King.'" *Victorian Poetry.* Ed. Malcolm Bradbury and David Palmer. New York: Crane, 89-121.

Hyder, Clyde K. *Swinburne Replies.* Syracuse: Syracuse University Press, 1966.

Jones, W. Lewis. *King Arthur in History and Legend.* Cambridge: Cambridge University Press, 1911.

Kennedy, Edward Donald, ed. *King Arthur: A Casebook.* New York: Garland, 1996.

Kindrick, Robert L. "The Administration of Justice in Malory's *Works.*" *Arthurian Interpretations* II (1987): 63-82.

Kirchoff, Frederick. *William Morris: The Construction of a Male Self, 1856-1972.* Athens, OH: Ohio University Press, 1990.

Lacy, Norris J., ed. *The Arthurian Encyclopedia.* New York: Bedrick, 1987.

La Farge, Catherine. "Conversation in Malory's *Morte Darthur.*" *Medium Ævum* 56 (1987): 225-38.

Lagorio, Valerie and Mildred Leake Day, eds. *King Arthur through the Ages.* New York: Garland, 1990.

Lang, Cecil. *The Pre-Raphaelites and Their Circle.* 2nd ed.Chicago: University of Chicago Press, 1975.

Loomis, Roger Sherman. *The Development of Arthurian Romance.* New York: Norton, 1970.

Lumiansky, R. M. "Sir Thomas Malory's *Le Morte Darthur*, 1947-1987: Author, Title, Text." *Speculum* 62 (1987): 878-97.

---, ed. *Malory's Originality.* Baltimore: Johns Hopkins University Press, 1964.

Maas, Jeremy. *Victorian Painters.* New York: Harrison, 1988.

MacCallum, Sir Mungo William. *Tennyson's "Idylls of the King"and Arthurian Story from the XVIth Century.* Freeport, NY: Books for Libraries, 1971.

Mackail, J. W. *The Life of William Morris.* 2 vols. New York: Longmans, 1907.

McGann, Jerome J. *Swinburne: An Experiment in Criticism.* Chicago: University of Chicago Press, 1972.

McGonagle, Declan. *William Morris Today.* London: Journeyman, 1984.

McGuire, Ian. "Epistemology and Empire in *Idylls of the King.*" *Victorian Poetry* 30. 3-4 (Autumn-Winter 1992): 387-400.

McSweeney, Kerry. *Tennyson and Swinburne as Romantic Naturalists.* Toronto: University of Toronto Press, 1981.

---. "The Structure of Swinburne's *Tristram of Lyonesse.*" *Queen's Quarterly* 75 (1968): 680-702.

Mancoff, Debra. *The Arthurian Revival in Victorian Art.* New York: Garland, 1990.

Marsh, Jan. *Pre-Raphaelite Women.* New York: Harmony, 1988. Marsh, Jan and Pamela Gerrish Nunn. *Women Artists and the Pre-Raphaelite Movement.* London: Virago, 1989.

Martin, Robert Bernard. *Tennyson: The Unquiet Heart.* Oxford: Clarendon, 1980.

Matthews, William. *The Tragedy of Arthur.* Berkeley: University Of California Press, 1960.

Maynadier, Howard. *The Arthur of the English Poets.* Boston: Houghton, 1907.

Miyoshi, Masao. "Narrative Sequence and the Moral System: Three Tristram Poems."*Victorian Newsletter* 35 (1969): 5-10.

Morgan, Thäis E. "Swinburne's Dramatic Monologues; Sex and Ideology." *Victorian Poetry* 22 (1984): 175-95.

Morris, Rosemary. *The Character of King Arthur in Medieval Literature.* Totowa, NJ: Rooman, 1982.

Oberg, Charlotte H. *A Pagan Prophet: William Morris.* Charlottesville: Unversity Press of Virginia, 1978.

Parris, Leslie, ed. *Pre-Raphaelite Papers.* London: Tate Gallery, 1984.

Perrine, Lawerence. "Morris's Guenevere: An Interpretation." *Philological Quarterly* 39 (1960): 234-41.

Pointon, Marcia, ed. *Pre-Raphaelites Re-Viewed.* Manchester: Manchester University Press, 1989.

Pratt, Linda Ray. "Matthew Arnold and the Modernist Image." *Matthew Arnold in His Time and Ours: Centenary Essays.* Ed. Clinton Machann and Forrest D. Burt. Charlottesville: University Press of Virginia, 1988. 81-97.

Priestley, F. E. L. "Tennyson's 'Idylls.'" *University of Toronto Quarterly* 19 (1949): 35-49.

Raymond, Meredith B. "The Arthurian Group in *The Defence of Guenevere and Other Poems.*" *Victorian Poetry* 4 (1966): 213-18.

Reed, John R. "Swinburne's *Tristram of Lyonesse*: The Poet-Lovers Song of Love." *Victorian Papers* 4 (1966): 99-120.

Reynolds, Graham. *Victorian Painting.* New York: Harper, 1987.

Ricks, Christopher, ed. *A Collection of Poems by Alfred Tennyson.* Garden City, NY: Doubleday, 1972.

Riede, David G. *Swinburne: A Study of Romantic Mythmaking.* Charlottesville: University Press of Virginia, 1978.

Roberts, Helene. "Divided Self, Divided Realm: Typology, History, and Persona in Tennyson's Idylls of the King." In *Pre-Raphaelitism and Medievalism in the Arts.* Ed. Liana De Girolami Cheyney. New York: Mellen, 1992. 29-52.

Roper, Alan H. "The Moral Landscape of Arnold's Poetry." *PMLA* 77 (1962): 289-96.

Rose, Andrea. *The Pre-Raphaelites.* 2nd ed. 1977. Oxford: Phaidon, 1981.

Rosenberg, John D. *The Fall of Camelot: A Study of Tennyson's "Idylls of the King."* Cambridge: Harvard University Press, 1973.

---. "Swinburne." *Victorian Studies* 9 (1967): 131-52.

Russ, Jon R. "A Possible Source for the Death Scene in Arnold's "Tristram and Iseult.'" *Victorian Poetry* 9 (1971): 336-38.

Sambrook, James. *Pre-Raphaelitism: A Collection of Critical Essays.* Chicago: University of Chicago Press, 1974.

Schwartz, Sanford. "Stitching and Unstitching Camelot: Narrative Transitions in Tennyson's *Idylls.*" *Philological Quarterly* 68.1 (Winter 1989): 77-100.

Serner, Gunnar. *On the Language of Swinburne's Lyrics and Epics.* Lund: Berlingska Boktryckeriet, 1910.

Shires, Linda M. "Patriarchy, Dead Men, and Tennyson's *Idylls of the King.*" *Victorian Poetry* 30:3-4 (Autumn-Winter 1992): 401-19.

Sillars, S. J. "Tristan and Tristram: Resemblance or Influence?" *Victorian Papers* 19 (1981): 81-86.

Silver, Carol. *The Romance of William Morris*. Athens, OH: Ohio University Press, 1982.

---. "In Defensc of Guenevere." *The Pre-Raphaelite Poets*. Ed. Harold Bloom. New York: Chelsea House, 1986. 134-47.

Simmons, Clare A. *Reversing the Conquest*. New Brunswick, NJ: Rutgers University Press, 1990.

Simpson, Arthur L., Jr. "Elaine the Unfair, Elaine the Unlovable: The Socially Destructive Artist/Woman in *Idylls of the King*." *Modern Philology* 89.3 (Feb. 1992): 341-62.

Simpson, Roger. *Camelot Regained*. Cambridge, Eng.: Brewer, 1990.

Smith, Elton Edward. *The Two Voices: A Tennyson Study*. Lincoln: University of Nebraska Press, 1964.

Snider, Clifton. "Merlin in Victorian Poetry: A Jungian Analysis." *Victorian Newsletter* 72 (1987): 51-59.

Staines, David. "Morris' Treatment of His Medieval Sources in *The Defence of Guenevere and Other Poems*." *Studies in Philology* 70 (1973); 439-64.

---. "Swinburne's Arthurian World." *Studia Neophilologica* 30 (1978): 53-70.

Stallman, Robert L. "The Lovers'   Progress: An Investigation of William Morris' 'The Defence of Guenevere' and 'King   Arthur's Tomb.'" *Studies in English Literature, 1500-1900* 15 (1975); 657-70.

Stange, G. Robert. *Matthew Arnold: The Poet as Humanist*. Princeton: Princeton University Press, 1967.

Stein, Richard L. "The Pre-Raphaelite Tennyson." *Victorian Studies* 24 (1981): 279-301.

Stephenson, Will, and Mimosa Stephenson. "Proto-Modernism in Tennyson's 'The Holy Grail.'" *Quondam et Futurus* 2.4 (Winter 1992): 49-55.

Stevenson, Catherine Barnes. "How It Struck a Contemporary: Tennyson's 'Lancelot and Elaine' and Pre-Raphaelite Art." *Victorian Newsletter* 60 (1981): 8-14.

Stevenson, Lionel. *The Pre-Raphaelite Poets*. New York: Norton, 1972.

Struve, Laura. "The Public Life and Private Desires of Women in William Morris's 'Defence of Guenevere.'" *Arthuriana* 6.3 (Fall 1996): 15-28.

Sylvia, Richard A. "Sexual Politics and Narrative Method in Tennyson's 'Guinevere.'" *Victorian Newsletter* 76 (Fall 1989): 23-28.

Sypher, Francis Jacques. "Swinburne and Wagner." *Victorian Papers* 9 (1971): 165-83.

Tate Gallery. *The Tate Gallery, 1984-86: Illustrated Catalogue of Acquisitions*. London: Tate Gallery Publications, 1988.

Taylor, Ina. *Victorian Sisters*. Bethesda, MD: Adler, 1987.

Thomas, Donald. *Swinburne: The Poet in His World*. New York: Oxford University Press, 1979.

Thompson, E. P. *William Morris: Romantic to Revolutionary*. New York: Pantheon, 1955.

Tredell, Nicholas. "*Tristran of Lyonesse*: Dangerous Voyage." *Victorian Papers* 20 (1982): 97-111.

Tucker, Herbert F. "The Epic Plight of Troth in *Idylls of the King*." *ELH* 58.3 (Fall 1991): 701-20.

---. "Trials of Fiction: Novel and Epic in the Geraint and Enid Episodes from *Idylls of the King*." *Victorian Poetry* 30.3-4 (Autumn-Winter 1992): 441-61.

Tucker, T. G. *The Foreign Debt of English Literature*. New York: Haskell, 1966.

Umland, Rebecca. "The Snake in the Woodpile: Tennyson's Vivien as Victorian Prostitute." *Culture and the King: The Social Implications of the Arthurian Legend*. Ed. Martin B. Schictman and James P. Carley. Albany: State University of New York Press, 1994. 274-87.

Ven-Ten Bensel, Elise Francisca Wilhelmina Maria van der. *The Character of King Arthur in English Literature*. New York: Haskell, 1966.

Vinaver, Eugène, ed. *The Works of Sir Thomas Malory*. 3 vols. continuously paged. Oxford: Clarendon University Press, 1987.

Whiteley, Jon. *Pre-Raphaelite Paintings and Drawings*. Oxford: Phaidon, 1989.

Winwar, Frances. *Poor Splendid Wings: The Rossettis and Their Circle*. Boston: Little, 1933.

Wood, Christopher. *The Pre-Raphaelites*. London: Weidenfeld, 1981.

Zesmer, David M. *Guide to English Literature--From "Beowulf" to Chaucer and Medieval Drama*. New York: Barnes, 1961.

Index

About the Authors

LAURA COONER LAMBDIN is an independent scholar and was formerly Assistant Professor of English at Francis Marion University. She has published on Malory, Chaucer, and various Victorian poets in such journals as *Philological Quarterly* and *Arthurian Interpretations*. With Robert Thomas Lambdin, she has edited *Chaucer's Pilgrims: An Historical Guide to the Pilgrims in "The Canterbury Tales"* (1996) and the *Encyclopedia of Medieval Literature* (2000), both available from Greenwood Press.

ROBERT THOMAS LAMBDIN is Assistant Professor of English in the Transitional Year in the College of Applied Sciences Program at the University of South Carolina. He has published several articles on medieval literature and is the coeditor of *Chaucer's Pilgrims: An Historical Guide to the Pilgrims in "The Canterbury Tales"* (1996) and the *Encyclopedia of Medieval Literature* (2000), both available from Greenwood Press.